BEST CRUISE TIPS

303 CRUISE HACKS SAVING YOU TIME, MONEY & FRUSTRATION

RANDALL STEWART

THE STEWART EDGE PUBLISHING

CONTENTS

INTRODUCTION

Imagine being able to visit other countries without having to unpack and pack at each destination. Of being able to participate in a myriad of onboard activities and never get bored. Or enjoy being pampered on a floating, all-inclusive resort. Cruising is an Art. Cruising can take you to fun, memorable, exotic destinations. There are a host of hacks and tips that can enhance your cruise vacation. Each cruise book that you read - and this is no exception - provides you with a different perspective on how to make the most out of your cruise vacation.

What's different about this particular guide is that it's designed to be quick reading, without a lot of extraneous material or what is affectionately known as fluff. I realize that not every cruise hack in this guide is going to resonate with you. That's why there are so many of them to choose from. Being able to quickly assess which one's could save you time, money and frustration is the ultimate goal as to how this guide is organized in this way. Not to mention being an entertaining read - to boot.

I've tapped into four decades of cruise experience in order to provide you with some interesting insights into how to make the most of your cruise vacation. Yes. I'm that old. Back in the day, when I was knee high to a grasshopper, I was fortunate enough to travel extensively as the cruise industry was taking shape. Fortunately, every year I continue to do so. The cruise industry has experienced dramatic changes in the last decade with the advent of online booking, massive cruise ships, amenities galore and onshore facilities that make cruising a real adventure and pleasure.

You're about to embark on a new adventure as you peruse through this guide. My fervent wish is that you embrace cruising as a preferred vacation option as much as my wife Cindy and I do. As you know, we can't make any promises as to how much money you could save by following these tips. Promises are like babies. They're fun to make but harder to deliver. However, you should be able to use several of these hacks to achieve this primary objective. So, without further ado, let's dive right into those 303 cruise tips and hacks.

1

SELECTING YOUR CRUISE

With so many choices available for going on a cruise vacation, it can be daunting trying to select one that'll suit your personality, needs and expectations. The following cruise hacks should steer you in the right direction before booking that first cruise experience. Ultimately, you want to create lasting memories that you can share with others after your awesome adventure. Here are 303 cruise tips to get you thinking - starting with how to pick your cruise.

Tip #1: Go on a Taster Cruise
Unsure as to whether cruising is going to be your cup of tea? Consider going on a shorter cruise that's less than 4 days long. This'll give you an opportunity to feel out a particular brand and cruise experience. Should you love the experience, you now have an opportunity to commit to a longer cruise. If your cruise was a bust, you haven't spent too much money. You may even be able to get some of your money back as some cruise lines offer a money-back guarantee for first-time cruisers.

Tip #2: Current Price Trends.

Cruises in the Caribbean have a lot of competition, especially with new cruise ships being added every year. Prices tend to be lower here than other parts of the world. Also, prices tend to rise much slower than the rate of inflation in this competitive Caribbean market. To take advantage of this price trend, consider booking a cruise on an older ship (more than 3 years old). Newer ships tend to command a higher price point, whereas older ships can offer you more competitive rates. Of recent note is that Alaskan cruises are experiencing a price trend increase. High demand, a short sailing season (peak season in June to mid-July) and limited port capacity favor the cruise lines. Traveling to Alaska? Ensure that you book well in advance and expect to pay premium rates.

Tip #3: Sardines Anyone?

Don't make the common mistake of cramming too many people into a cabin. Having four cabin mates in two bunkbeds and a cabin the size of a walk-in closet is a recipe for disaster. Sure, you might save some money. But when you're packed in so tight like a can of sardines, ask yourself: Where the heck do we put all the bags and clothing? Your cramped cabin can quickly turn into the most uncomfortable place on the ship - that is next to shacking up in the bilge.

Tip #4: What Do You Desire?

People on the same ship as you want different things, whether that be privacy, good food, a party atmosphere, fun onboard activities or comfortable conditions. Match your cruise ship to the experiences you desire. First, jot down all those aspects of a vacation that are important to you. Then, prioritize your list of what's most important. Next, check out online reviews to better match your priorities with a particular cruise ship/ line. One popular review site is **CruiseMates.com**. Also, check with your cruise agent should you be using one.

Tip #5: Keeping Track with a Spread Sheet.
As you begin exploring various cruise options, you'll want to set up an easily-referenced list of potential cruises to keep tabs on. By using an electronic spreadsheet or word processor, you can quickly compare your research results. At a minimum, keep track of your options by using a notebook for the purpose of scheduling your cruise. Being organized makes it that much easier to plan your vacation, wouldn't you agree?

Tip #6: Select Your Cruise Line Very Carefully.
Cruise lines abound and each one is trying to attract a different target market. Knowing which brands will best meet your needs is the first step to planning a great vacation. Spending some time identifying what you would like to get out of your cruise vacation goes a long way in matching the right onboard experience with your expectations.

The two largest ocean cruise companies are Carnival and Royal Caribbean. Carnival is the largest with a portfolio of brands such as Cunard, Holland America, Seabourn, Costa and Carnival. Each offers different experiences, service levels and onboard features. In general, Carnival offers cruisers the most activities compared to its competitors. Norwegian tends to be the least regimented in their approach. Both Royal Caribbean and Princess tend to have slightly better food options.

Should you be looking at a river cruise the 3 largest providers are Viking, Uniworld and Ama Waterways. Each offers a slightly different level of service and luxury.
Top of the line luxury brands include Regent Seven Seas, Crystal

Cruises and Celebrity. While more popular less expensive lines include Princess, Royal Caribbean and Carnival. A little online research will help you better understand what each option has to offer to meet your particular tastes. A cruise-expert travel agent, online cruise forums and blogs can provide you with greater insights into what is and isn't for you. To learn more about each of these cruise lines visit **CruiseDirect.com**, which focuses on selling cruises only.

Tip #7: Never Book a Cruise Based Solely on Price.

Your booking decision should take into account travel to and from the cruise, hotel rooms, incidental travel expenses, the cruise itinerary, the ship's reputation and the target audience the cruise line is trying to attract. All of these factors should be a part of the planning process in order to get the most out of your vacation. Cheaping it out may save you money upfront, but at what cost down the road?

Tip #8: Multiply Your Options.

Just as you would probably not buy the first car you see on the lot, so should you take some time to do your due diligence on cruise options available to you. Why pay 20 or 30% more for a cruise when you can let your fingers do the heavy lifting. Get multiple quotes from various sources before you buy, whether it be with the cruise line, travel sites like **CruiseDeals.com, BookingBuddy.com, Cayole.com, CruiseCritic.com** or **VacationsToGo.com** or from a "cruise expert" travel agent. As a side note, your travel agent should not charge you any booking or incidental fees. Run for the door if they mention it.

Tip #9: Choose Your Sailing Date and Itinerary Carefully.

Keep in mind that different types of cruises appeal to specific target groups. For example, short cruises under a week long tend to attract a younger crowd, while longer cruises are very popular with old farts like me.

You'll find that periods around school holidays such as spring break are most suited to families. And, some ships like Disney are more family friendly than others with activities and extensive child minding services specially catered to the young ones. The last thing you want if you're going on family cruise with youngsters is to be booked onto a party cruise full of rowdy college students or rambunctious seniors whooping it up on Geritol.

Tip #10: Peak Season, Shoulder Season, Off Season - Oh My!
For cheaper rates, consider booking at the beginning or end of the typical "peak" cruise season. This is known as the shoulder season. Most cruise lines realize that in order to attract cruise passengers when the weather isn't the most ideal, they need to offer reduced fares. If excursions in your ports of call are not a priority, then this may be a viable option for you, especially on the larger cruise ships that have a gazillion activities to do on board. Check out the **CruiseCritic.com** website for specific suggestions.

Tip #11: Where is Everyone in Town?
Prior to booking your cruise, check the dates of each port of call you'll be visiting to see if any major local holidays are scheduled. You may find most of the shops and attractions closed outside of the cruise terminal area itself. Knowing in advance what to expect will be less frustrating. It'll also give you time to plan alternative activities should this be the case.

Tip #12: Are You a Frequent Smoker?
You may wish to book a balcony suite if the cruise line allows smoking on the balcony. Check beforehand. There are very few places where you can indulge on the ship. You may find it

inconvenient to always head up to a designated smoking area like the casino or starboard (right) side of the Promenade deck on most ships. Just don't make the fatal mistake of smoking in your cabin, it could cost you an arm and a leg to remove the smoke smell form your cabin. And you don't want to be hobbling off the ship, do you?

Tip #13: Save Money. Book an Inside Cabin.
If you know you'll be spending little time in your cabin, then selecting an inside cabin that doesn't have any views can save you upwards of 60% compared to a balcony suite. This is a popular option for the younger crowd and first-time cruisers on a budget.

Tip #14: The Best Cabin for Value?
In a nutshell, an inside cabin generally offers the best value if you don't intend on spending a lot of time in your cabin other than for dressing and sleeping. The room layout and size is similar for an inside cabin as it is for one that has a window or balcony. Sure, you may end up with a few square feet of extra room with a balcony suite; however, that difference could cost you a pretty penny - or an ugly one for that matter.

Tip #15: Balcony Cabin Selection. What Side of the Ship?
Before booking your cabin, check out your cruise ship's itinerary on a map. If the ship is heading in a clockwise circle, book a balcony cabin on the left-hand (port) side. Should the ship be moving in a counter-clockwise direction, book on the right-hand (starboard) side of the ship. This way you'll have a view of the coast as you're sailing into and out of the various ports of call.

Tip #16: Save on a Balcony Suite.
Some balcony suites have partially obstructed views because of the lifeboats. The obstruction is usually not that bad. Do some

research on the cruise lines website and see if you can find some pictures of the obstructed views on your particular ship. You could end up getting a beautiful balcony room at a significantly lower rate.

Tip #17: Avoid New Cruise Ship Hype.
Don't buy into the hype and increased selling price point that is often marketed to unsuspecting first-time cruisers thinking they'll miss out on certain amenities or features. All cruise ships offer all of the most popular amenities. So, a well-maintained cruise ship that is several years old won't disappoint you in any appreciable way. What'll bring a smile to your face, is having a similar experience at a fraction of the hyped price. Wouldn't that be better than a poke in the eye with a sharp stick?

Tip #18: Watch Out for Price Scams.
A common cruise scam is seeing listed prices that seem too good to be true. Prices that appear to be much lower than any other vendor. U.S. taxes and fees are generally included in the list price. Port charges and port taxes may not be. Avoid a rude awakening by asking the provider what the "total" cost of the cruise would be including all taxes and fees. You want to know upfront what your entire total price will be. Make a point of asking up front in advance.

Tip #19: Handicapped Access Cabins.
You must book early if you have any hopes of getting one, which is usually based on a first come first served basis. These cabins need to be booked through either a travel agent or online representative who'll assess whether or not you have significant health or mobility challenges. You'll need to provide a medical document filled in by your physician that specifies the nature of your mobility problem.

Tip #20: Cruising with a Large Party?
Plan far in advance. If you're traveling with a diverse group that has varying needs and expectations, do your research early. This enables you to identify a "best fit" cruise ship and itinerary. Now, you'll have a better chance of selecting a cruise that meets all of the main priorities your group desires.

Tip #21: What's Your Ship's Reputation?
Every cruise ship is unique, even if they represent the same brand. Before you book your vacation, you need to be aware of what facilities and amenities there are onboard that particular cruise ship. An easy way to do so, is to check out what other cruisers say about that ship on **CruiseCritic.com** where you can view photos, read reviews and get a sense of what the personality of the ship might be. Social media can be helpful in this regard.

Tip #22: Weather or Not!
Other than hurricane season in the Caribbean, which is typically from June 1 to November 30, weather is typically good. Even if you book at the beginning or end of the hurricane season, often the worst-case scenario is that your cruise ship will re-route to a different destination. Should you be travelling to Alaska, the weather is cold until mid-May and rainy after mid-July. And cruises up the east coast of The Excited States are best planned for the warmer summer months or in late September when the fall colors offer a spectacular backdrop while cruising.

Tip #23: Typical Weather at Ports of Call.
Prior to booking any cruise, verify the average monthly temperature of each of the ports of call you'll be visiting. You can use **Weather.com** or **TheWeatherNetwork.com** to get a feel for what you'll encounter as far as average temperatures and

precipitation. This'll enable you to better pack for the weather patterns you may encounter on your cruise. Makes sense, right?

Tip #24: Choosing Your Departure Port.
Traveling from afar? Your choice of a departure port for your cruise could save you a lot of money. Most cruises originate from the southern states in the U.S. And the top three U.S. ports are Miami, Fort Lauderdale and Cape Canaveral. Flights to each of these departure ports can vary significantly. Choose your jump off point with this in mind. The same applies to cruises out of Los Angeles and New York.

Tip #25: Damn! We Missed Our Embarkation by an Hour.
Yes, it happens. If you are traveling from afar, avoid flying the same day your cruise departs. Airlines are not 100% reliable. Even a minor weather or mechanical delay could cost you your trip or add to the cost of your vacation. We like to give ourselves a buffer day to get to our ship. Not only does it give us peace of mind, but we can also better acclimate to the sub-tropical weather when arriving from a winter wonderland. At a minimum, schedule your arrival time at least five hours before your cruise departure, since most insurance companies won't issue a refund for delays less than five hours long.

~

2

GETTING A GOOD PRICE

How do you get a good price on a cruise? Deals can be had at any price point you are considering. The following tips and strategies will have you thinking about how to go about finding those gems.

Tip #26: Never Pay the List Price.
A cabin's "list price" varies based on the time left before departure, the current booking capacity and the competition in the market. To get a better deal, do a little research in advance. If you're flexible, booking just a week before or after peek weeks such as around Christmas or Spring Break can be advantageous. You may be able to save 40 - 50 % off the list price, rather than pay a premium.

Tip #27: Wanting a Dirt-Cheap Cruise?
If you're able to travel on short notice or are flexible, then this option may work out for you. First of all, you'll need to set your upper price limit for your cruise, such as less than $75 per day, per person for the cruise. Next, limit your search. Avoid looking at any cruises above your set price. Then, become an expert in finding

low-priced cruises by using travel search engines and following
the tips and strategies outlined in this guide.

Tip #28: The Least Expensive Cruises?

Cruises to the Caribbean tend to offer the consumer the best bang
for their buck. This is due to the fierce competition amongst the
top dogs in the industry. If you're considering a first-time cruise
and are budget conscious, explore those cruise options that target
destinations in the Caribbean. We've never been disappointed.

Tip #29: Book with a Credit Card, Not Debit.

It's better to pay for cruises, hotels and travel with a credit card
rather than using cash from your piggy bank, personal checks,
traveler's checks, money transfers, a debit card or cryptocurrency.
All credit card companies offer some degree of protection against
fraud or loss, should the agency you're dealing with fail to deliver.
Contact your credit card company directly to see what your card
covers for vacation protection. You may be pleasantly surprised.

Tip #30: Book All Cabins at Once.

Most cabins are designed to comfortably accommodate two
people. However, should you be looking at adding another
roommate or two, do so when you make your initial booking. Not
only will the rates be slightly less, but any incentives or discounts
would apply to all of your cabin mates. Adding a person later on
or at the last minute could cost you significantly. Be aware that
rooms with beds for more than two people are not that common.
Expect them to book up fast. So, start checking on it as soon as
you know what cruise you'll be going on.

Tip #31: Use a Bottom Up Approach for Cabin Selection.

Cruise ships have four general categories of cabins priced from
lowest to highest, namely:

- Inside Cabin (no window).
- Outside Cabin (window or porthole outside).
- Balcony Cabin.
- Suite.

Cabin pricing is also a function of location with the lower decks being less expensive than the upper ones and mid-ship being more desirable than the front or back. If you're motivated to get the best deal on a cabin, start by looking at Inside Cabins located on the lower decks. Once you identify some options, check out deck floor plans below and above your deck to see if you'll be inconvenienced in any way by noise coming from mechanical equipment, onboard entertainment, foot traffic, elevators, or even us whooping it up and dancing on the tables in the lounge above you.

Tip #32: How to Get the Best Quotes? Haggle!
Doing research on the Internet for prices only goes so far. To get the absolute best deals on a cabin, call providers and haggle. Yes, pick up the phone and ask for any and all discounts that might apply. But before you do so, arm yourself with information about those particular cruises you would like to go on. You're more likely to get a better deal if you show the agent that you've done your homework in advance.

Tip #33: Don't Be Fooled by the Claims.
Many websites will claim that they have the best prices. Some of them even offer a guarantee, which unfortunately ends up being more of a sales gimmick than anything else. Be aware that no provider consistently has all the best prices. Do your due diligence in advance by shopping around. You'll start to recognize a deal when you see it by visiting various sources.

Tip #34: Is that Per Person or Per Cabin?
Should you be offered a discount or onboard credits for selecting a particular cruise, verify which scenario applies. Most cabin discounts are based on a per person rate, while onboard credits are often applied to the entire cabin. Knowing this allows you to compare offers and make a more educated decision as to which offer is potentially better.

Tip #35: Understand and Watch the Extras.
Over the past decade less and less of what used to be more of an all-inclusive cruise experience is slowly evolving. Your cruise ticket is inclusive of lodging, basic food and most activities. However, if you would like to dine in an upscale restaurant, pamper yourself in the spa, grab a glass of wine, get photos of you and your loved one or treat yourself to an espresso and slice of chocolate torte you'll need to ante up. On average consider budgeting 50 - 60% of your cruise ticket for onboard incidentals. And to avoid any price shock at the end of your trip, plan ahead, set a budget and monitor your daily expenditures.

Tip #36: All Those Extras Cost. Buyer Beware.
Cruise lines make a killing by selling their captive audience, that's you, all sorts of services and amenities beyond your basic accommodation, food and entertainment that is covered in your initial booking. Cruise lines count on you spending additional money. Most services are going to be at a premium compared to what you would pay at home. If a haircut is just a haircut, get one before you travel. The same rule applies to any other onboard extras. Sure, pick up a copy of that photo of you and your loved one dancing on the tables with us right next to you. Just be cautious as to how the cruise lines make their money.

Tip #37: Fuel Surcharges, Should I be Worried?

Most cruise lines do not impose a fuel surcharge that is based on a fixed price point for crude oil, usually around $65 per barrel for West Texas Intermediate Crude. However, most lines do "reserve" the right to charge you. Some of the smaller lines like Cunard, P&O Lines and Fred Olsen Lines do charge a small surcharge. Most of the big players do not because of fierce competition in the market. Should the price of crude skyrocket in and around your booking, be proactive and budget for a possible surcharge of $10 per day, per person, that you'll be required to pay before disembarkation.

Tip #38: The Two Best Time Periods to Book.

Booking a year or so out from your cruise offers some of the best pricing available from the cruise lines. The sooner the cruise line is able to fill the ship the better off they are in terms of marketing endeavors. The second booking opportunity, if you're flexible (and I'm not talking about being a yogi), is to book at the last minute. It costs the cruise line the same amount for fixed costs whether the ship is at full capacity or not. Rather than sail with empty cabins they'll offer deep discounts just prior to sailing. However, keep in mind that most cruises do sell out and sail at 100% capacity. You may need to be aggressive in your research efforts to find those last-minute gems.

Tip #39: The Two Best Days to Book.

Around Thanksgiving on Black Friday and Cyber Monday, cruise lines typically offer the best deals of the year. They know consumers are looking for savings on their purchases and have gotten into the game by offering discounts, upgrades and onboard credits to incentivize you to book. Something to consider, right?

Tip #40: December Bookings.

The first two weeks of December tend to be less expensive than the last two weeks, should you be considering booking around the Christmas period. Cabin prices can vary a lot based on the popularity of certain cruise ships, your literary and of course the sailing dates. If you're flexible you may wish to take advantage of any late booking discounts for this shoulder season.

Tip #41: Keep Tabs on the Price You're Paying.

Should you book early, keep monitoring the price to see if you can get a better deal. Use websites like **Cruiseline.com** and **CruiseFareMonitor.com**. Also check out some of the paid and free apps like **CruiseDeals.com** and the **Ship Mate app**. Once you set a price alert, the platform will alert you as to any price changes. If you're within you're allowed cancelation period, you can take advantage of the lower price point. Often, you'll be able to receive an onboard credit or free upgrade by being vigilant.

Tip #42: NON-Refundable Deposits Are Commonplace.

It used to be that most cruise lines offered a full refund for bookings made up to 90 days or so before your cruise. This is no longer the norm. Many cruise lines have already moved to decrease the price volatility in their bookings and cancellations by charging fees for changing a booking. The bottom line? Don't expect to get a full refund from most cruise lines.

Tip #42: My Cabin's Guaranteed for What?

Guaranteed or "to be assigned" cabins offer you one of the cheapest booking options. The downside is that you may end up in a noisier or obstructed part of the ship should you book a balcony stateroom. On the upside, you could get bumped up a class/ deck. And of course, you'll benefit from the lower rates. To increase your chances of getting a better cabin, book early many months before the cruise.

Tip #43: Want to Cruise for Dirt Cheap?

Book in bulk. Most major cruise lines will offer onboard credits, upgrades and even free cruises when you book a large group of cabins usually with 10 or more bookings. Check out how you could benefit by contacting the cruise line directly or have your travel agent work on your behalf.

Tip #44: Belong to a Special Group?

You could be entitled to an additional discount of 5-10%. Most cruise lines offer specialty groups that are based on an affiliation, a profession, your age or the geographical region you hail from. Although most online booking systems will prompt you for this information, it doesn't hurt to enquire about your particular status. Doing so could lead to some additional savings. And that would be better than a kick in the pants with a frozen boot, wouldn't you agree?

Tip #45: Cruising with Carnival.

With Carnival being the big dog in the cruise industry and having so many berths to fill, they often offer great incentives for booking early, as in a year out. However, since they're challenged to fill all of their ships to maximum capacity, you can get great deals within a 3-month window prior to sailing. Keep an eye out for those special deals.

Tip #46: Cruising with Disney.

Expect to see discounts from Disney when you book your cruise a year or so in advance. Even though they expect to sell out long before the cruise, they like other cruise lines, like having more certainty as to their variable expenses and income.

Tip #47: Love Cruising? Book Your Next Cruise While Onboard.
I may be getting ahead of myself by mentioning this tip. Some of
the best rates available to you will be offered while you're on your
cruise. Discounts, onboard credits, reduced deposits, and even a
plastic ship replica on a stick may entice you into booking that
next cruise. Should you change your mind, dates can often be
switched or a refund issued with greater ease.

3

WHAT TO BOOK

Selecting the location of your cabin needn't be a daunting task. Given that we all have different needs, requirements and preferences, here's a list of cruise hacks that'll address the most pressing concerns.

Tip #48: Verify Who Your Neighbors Are.
We've made this rookie mistake before by booking a cabin right above the band playing in the casino. Fortunately, we were able to move to another cabin and get a decent night's sleep the next day. No need to make our mistake. Before booking your cabin, check out the floor plan of your cruise ship to get an idea as to what could be a serious distraction, such as an elevator, stairwell, orchestra pit, noisy laundry room, etc. And don't forget to check out both the deck above and below yours for potential problems.

Tip #49: Sensitive to Noise?
If you select a cabin at the front (forward) of the ship, pounding wave action could be a distractor. Should you select a cabin at the rear (aft) of the ship, motor sounds may be a problem. Choose

cabins that are located at the end of the hall or in middle of the ship on an upper deck if you would like less of a noise distraction. Balcony units can sometimes be a good choice, especially if you want to escape the constant barrage of music being piped over the speakers on deck on some cruise ships.

Tip #50: Sensitive to Motion Sickness?
Your best bet is to select a unit that is located in the middle of the ship and on a lower deck, where the perceived motion will be less. More on motion sickness hacks in tip #299.

Tip #51: Mobility Issues?
Look into getting a cabin that is centrally located and close to an elevator. This will minimize your travel distance from your cabin to other onboard locations and position you to take advantage of the elevators rather than trying to navigate the endless array of stairs.

Tip #52: Traveling with Kids?
Since many of the ship's activities are located in the top, rear (aft) section of the ship, consider booking a room close by. Your children will have an easier and more direct access to some of their favorite venues to hang out in.

Tip #53: Carnival's "Faster to the Fun" Option.
Purchase this $50 option (2019) as early as possible, should you be wanting priority boarding on your cruise. Not only could you end up benefitting from spending an extra couple of hours onboard before sailing, you'll also have priority check-in and delivery of your luggage, priority for spa and restaurant reservations and priority boarding for tenders. This option always sells out early; so, don't dilly-dally.

4

FINDING YOUR CRUISE

Where "should" you be looking to find the right cruise that'll save you money and time? The following cruise hacks will not only point you in the right direction, but also help reduce the stress of planning and preparing for your cruise vacation.

Tip #54: Use a Three-Pronged Attack.
Research is the key to finding your ideal cruise. Consider tapping into the following three great sources of information as you begin exploring your options:

1. An online discount search engine catering to cruise travel, such as **VacationsToGo.com**.
2. The online search capabilities offered by each individual cruise line's website.
3. A local "cruise expert" travel agent.

The more insights you can gain, the more confident you'll become in selecting the right cruise and itinerary.

Tip #55: Read Reviews with a Critical Eye.
All reviews are subjective. What appeals to one individual, may offend another. When sifting through reviews about a particular cruise ship, take all negative comments with a grain of salt. Look for general trends. If many people are commenting about the same issue on different cruise dates, then this is problematic.

Tip #56: Hiring a "Cruise Expert" Travel Agent.
Although you don't really need a travel agent to book a hotel room, cruises are a different beast all together. A "Cruise Expert" has intimate knowledge of the industry and can reduce the hassle factor when making all of your travel arrangements. They're able to do the extensive research needed to match your needs with the ideal cruise and offer you great deals on certain cruises, thus saving you money on your trip. Also, try to find a cruise specialist in your local region as they'll better understand your travel needs in getting to and from your port of departure. And don't worry about the cost of using a travel agent. They're not any more expensive than doing it yourself.

Tip #57: Ask Lots of Questions.
When dealing with either a local travel agent or one from an online powerhouse, ask a lot of questions about getting incentives, onboard gifts, upgrades, onboard ship credits, and different types of discounts. Travel agents aren't required to disclose all of the perks they have access to. Their goal is to have you book a cruise through them that makes you happy. By asking lots of questions, you increase the likelihood of getting the biggest bang for your buck. Wouldn't that be the cat's meow?

Tip #58: Post a Free Ad on CruiseMates.com.
Once on the **CruiseMates.com** website, do a quick registration. Then, click on "Bargain Finder" and post an anonymous ad,

asking for a cruise. Be very specific about what you want. List as much information about yourself, desired cruise line, dates, itinerary and other pertinent info. Travel agents can then get back to you with various offers that may be enticing. Not a bad hack at that!

Tip #59: Get Bids from CruiseCompete.com.

At **CruiseCompete.com** let them know what you're looking for in a cruise. They'll contact a number of travel agencies who'll get back to you with various offers. Select the bid that meets your priorities the best. But be prepared to act quickly, as these deals expire within a day or so.

Tip #60: Doing It Yourself?

Should you enjoy the thrill of the hunt, consider researching and booking your cruise online yourself. Once you've familiarized yourself with some of the cruise terms and language used in the industry, just follow the tips in this guide to plan and book your trip yourself. We often use this approach when we cruise since it allows us to explore different possibilities and gets us even more excited about our upcoming vacation. **VacationsToGo.com** is a comprehensive cruise search engine that'll potentially save you hundreds of dollars on a cruise. And **CruiseCritic.com** will give you some insights into the various cruise ships out there and what others are saying about their experiences.

Tip #61: The 90-Day Ticker.

VacationsToGo.com has a section of their website devoted to last minute deals. The "Find a Bargain" button will expose you to a number of incredible bargains that haven't sold out yet. The only challenge is ensuring that you can get a decent price on your airfare should you be traveling from abroad.

Tip #62: Read the Fine Print before Booking.
If you're booking your cruise online, take the time to go through all of the details as to what is included and what is exempt. Don't commit until you fully understand what you're agreeing to. And should you have any concerns or questions, contact the cruise line's help desk to clarify any issues.

Tip #63: Gain Peace of Mind with Insurance.
You may think that the added cost of travel and medical insurance is unnecessary for a cruise holiday since you'll be spending most of your time in a safe environment. However, insurance can compensate you should you have a travel delay, unforeseen emergency or health issues. When determining how much insurance to get, you should have enough to cover your non-refundable portions of your vacation as opposed to the total anticipated cost. Makes sure that you purchase your insurance within the appropriate time limit, which varies from 3 to 14 days after you make your first purchase. If you're working with a cruise-expert travel agent, have them bundle your insurance with other services to cut down on the cost. Expect to pay around 10% of the price of the cruise for travel insurance.

Tip #64: Third Party vs. Cruise Line Insurance.
To get the coverage you desire, consider booking with a 3rd party provider like Allianz, rather than insurance being offered through the cruise line. Cruise lines offer insurance packages stacked in their favor and not necessarily to your benefit. The only advantage of purchasing insurance through the cruise line is that many cruise lines will give you a 75% - 90% credit towards the cost of a future cruise.

Tip #65: Additional Health Insurance?
Hell, yes! Most people don't realize that their domestic health

insurance plans, won't cover them out of the country. Health care expenses outside of the country can be catastrophic. For a few dollars a day, you can eliminate that worry knowing that you'll be able to get the care you need without having to take a second mortgage out on your family home or sell your kids to the gypsies. Some popular providers to check out are **TravelexInsurance.com**, **TravelGuard.com** and **AllianzTravelInsurance.com**.

Tip #66: Free Insurance?

It's worthwhile to check with your credit card company to see what types of insurance they may be offering you should you book and pay for your adventure with that credit card. Most credit card companies offer some sort of travel insurance benefits for airline bookings, car rentals and hotel reservations. You may be pleasantly surprised to see what is covered, possibly saving you some money down the road. Now, wouldn't that make you happier than a clam at high tide?

Tip #67: Check the Gratuities Process.

Before setting sail, check to see if gratuities are included or excluded from your fare. You'll need to budget for this cost, which is about $11 per day per person. Most cruise lines will encourage you to pay a fee based on a fixed percentage of your ticket price. This tends to be the most common hassle-free option. Back 25 years ago, stuffing cash into envelopes was the norm. This is usually no longer the case with the ease of online booking. Makes it more convenient, wouldn't you agree?

Tip #68: What Else Can I Expect to Spend?

Besides the cost of getting to your cruise, your cruise itself, travel/ health insurance and gratuities, you'll also need to budget for other common vacation expenses. Most cruise lines offer you the option of booking a myriad of experiences online prior to sailing.

You can make restaurant and spa reservations, book excursions in ports of call, order special treats for your cabin, and even purchase wine, beer and soft drink packages. You'll also want to ensure that you have some cash on hand for tipping porters, drivers and guides. And don't forget to take your credit card and/or cash along when in port to pay for incidentals, such as souvenirs, photo packages and the occasional meal or cold beverage.

~

5

GETTING TO YOUR CRUISE

Should you have to fly to your cruise port and find accommodation for a night's stay, then these cruise hacks will help you get the best rates. We'll also have you arriving with plenty of time to board your cruise ship should you experience any travel delays.

Tip #69: Best Time to Book Your Flight?
According to **CheapAir.com** and The Huffington Post the best window of opportunity to book a flight is approximately 21 to 121 days in advance. The exception to this rule is if you'll be flying into Florida during spring break. In this case, book as early as possible. Airlines have no incentive to lower prices when demand is high. Contrary to popular opinion, there is no best day to "buy" your ticket.

Tip #70: Best Days to Fly?
Tuesdays and Wednesdays tend to be the cheapest days to actually fly. Fridays and Saturdays are often more expensive. Most cruise vacationers fly in a few hours to a day before their departure.

We've found that by flying in mid-week what we save on airfare pays for an extra night's stay at a hotel or AirBnB. That extra vacation time spent unwinding before our cruise makes our entire vacation that much more relaxing and memorable, wouldn't you agree?

Tip #71: Learn to Play the Booking Game.

Booking search engines are able to track your buying intentions by monitoring "cookies" that they set up on your computer when you search. I wish they would just send me normal cookies. They can also monitor the IP address (your computer's location) when you search. They know you would like to book a flight. So, the rates you see as you search over a period of time might be higher than what someone else might see for the first time. Avoid this hassle, by deleting any cookies in your computer after you've done a search. As well, use your smartphone to verify prices should you use a computer to do your investigating. Just make sure that you turn off your wireless access and just use a LTE or 4G connection.

Tip #72: Want the Best Price on Airfare?

Here's a simple 3-pronged approach to getting a good deal. Start by checking out major online travel sites like **Kayak.com**. Then, check with the cruise line and ask for their airfare price when booked with the cruise. Make sure that they give you an actual price as opposed to an approximate one. Next, contact a travel agent for their best price for the cruise and airfare combined. As a general rule of thumb, the more services you can bundle (cruise, airfare, hotel, car rental, etc.), the cheaper the entire package.

Tip #73: Search for Airline Promo Codes.

Before making your actual booking for your airline, do an Internet search for a discount promo code. Just type in the name of your airline, followed by "promo code". Be advised that this is a hit and miss strategy. When it does work, you'll be able to get a promotional code that'll save you 5% - 10% on your flight. Not a bad deal, wouldn't you say?

Tip #74: Consider Flying into Alternative Airports.
Should you be flying into major centers such as Los Angeles, New York or the Miami area, check out the price differences that may be offered by neighboring airports. Airfares are often more competitive for smaller airports that are close by major ones. Having saved on airfare, now it's just a matter of catching a shuttle or transfer to the cruise port. This can work exceptionally well when departing from Miami and flying into Fort Lauderdale.

Tip #75: Fly into Port as Early as Possible.
Try to arrive in your departure port city as soon as you can, especially when traveling in the winter. Arriving a day in advance allows you to start a mini-vacation before your cruise. Should there be a travel delay, you'll at least have an opportunity to still make your cruise connection the next day. We always arrive a day or two before our cruise. There's nothing like peace of mind before embarking on a new adventure.

Tip #76: Fly in the Morning.
Flying in the morning gives you an extra cushion of time should you run into travel delays. It's much easier to take an alternative flight or route to get to your destination if the airlines have most of the day to work on it. The added bonus is that you'll have more time to kick back or explore your destination city.

Tip #77: Avoid a Missed Flight.
For $19 (for each leg) you can insure your U.S. flight with the **Freebird** app. This service notifies you if your flight gets cancelled

or delayed. And it provides you with booking options on every airline so you can get out on the next flight.

Tip #78: Arrive Early at the Airport.

Should you be flying into your debarkation port, ensure that you arrive at the airport at least two hours before your flight. This enables you to deal with any unforeseen emergencies or delays in getting to the airport. Not only that, it gives you time to relax and unwind at the airport knowing that you're unrushed. There's nothing worse than running around the house like a chicken with its head cut off, scrambling last minute trying to get out the door to catch your flight.

Tip #79: Book Your Return Flight for after Noon.

Most cruise ships begin the disembarkation process after 8 a.m. However, by the time you clear Homeland Security you may be pushing 9 a.m. or even 10 a.m. This places additional travel stress on you should you have an early flight. Your best bet? Book an afternoon flight. Now you can have a leisurely breakfast and relax a bit before heading off to the airport.

Tip #80: Ask for Tour Operator Prices.

Tour operator prices may be available to you when you make multiple bookings for your vacation such as a combination of airfare, hotel reservations and car rentals. This is one way that these providers can discount their prices without actually having to post discounted rates online. The catch? In many cases you must enquire about getting a "tour operator" price. It's well worth it, especially if you can get a hotel and car rental for cheaper than a hotel room on its own.

Tip #81: Consider the Cruise Line's Transfer Service.

We almost always pre-book an airport transfer through the cruise line when we make our initial reservations. The modest fee charged assures us that we'll get to the airport on time while riding in the comfort of an air-conditioned coach.

Tip #82: Save Money on Taxis.
Both Uber and Lyft offer a cost-saving alternative to paying for a taxi. The rates are significantly less and the service comparable. Just download the free mobile app for the provider and set up an account. You can usually get a $15 - $20 credit for your first ride. Now, that's nothing to sneeze at!

Tip #83: A Hotel Room for Less?
Consider using the services of the **AirBnB** network. AirBnB is a short-term rental option of a private apartment or home. This can be a cost-effective way of staying in your departure port the night before your cruise.

Tip #84: Set on Staying in a Hotel?
Use a search engine like **Hotels.com** or another that'll offer free cancellation up to 24 hours in advance. Book your room, then periodically search for a cheaper or better alternative. You can always cancel your reservation should you find a gem of a deal. Also, ask for "the lowest possible price" rather than the "best price" should you be talking to an agent. Using the correct terminology could save you a few bucks.

Tip #85: Avoid Getting Robbed.
When staying at a hotel, place a "Do Not Disturb" sign on your doorknob when you head out of the room. Most thieves will assume that someone is in the room and move on to the next potential target.

Tip #86: Are You an Amazon Prime Member?
If so, you can have local restaurants deliver to you for free. This beats pricey room service. And the food choices are better. If you're not an Amazon Prime member the first month is free and $12.99 a month thereafter. Something to consider investing in, right?

∾

6

PACKING YOUR BAGS

There's an art to packing your bags so that you're traveling light and everything is easy to find and hang up once you're onboard. In this chapter, you'll pick up a number of tips that'll show you how to properly pack your suitcases and carry-on bags specifically for cruising.

Tip #87: Be an Officer Check-Off.
Using a packing checklist designed with cruising in mind, helps you stay organized. A simple Internet search should reveal a number of free, downloadable options for you. Look for one that allows you to add items not mentioned as I'm sure some of the tips in this guide won't be included. Packing is a very personal and individual affair. Unfortunately, most checklists can only provide you with a good start in planning your trip. Individualizing it to meet your specific needs will be the first order of business.

Tip #88: What to Pack in Your Carry-On Luggage.
Since the whole embarkation process takes time, don't expect to receive your checked luggage for several hours. Be proactive, by

packing those items you'll need to enjoy the onboard action in your carry-on bag. Have your swimwear, a set of spare clothes, water sandals/ flip flops, medication, valuables, electronics, chargers/power bars and even a bottle of your favorite wine with you upon embarkation. This minimizes the chance of your checked bag being held back for inspection.

Tip #89: How Much Luggage to Take?
Since cabin space may be at a premium, I recommend taking a maximum of three pieces of luggage per couple. For example, we usually travel with one checked bag and two lightweight carry-on bags. Most airlines will allow carry-on bags that are under 22" x 14" x 9". If you're using packing systems that'll consolidate your travel items, you could even get away with two carry-on bags. We spent 10 days sailing along the Mexican coast doing this. The fewer the pieces of luggage to deal with, the easier it is to manage, wouldn't you agree?

Tip #90: Purse or Backpack?
Although you may be tempted to take a large purse with you on your vacation, a second alternative may be more practical and provide you with more options. By taking a small, collapsible backpack you'll be able to:

1. take this on an airplane as a personal bag, plus be able to take a carry-on bag.
2. pack your pool side items and be able to free up your hands should you be standing in line at the food buffet.
3. use it for any excursion or beach adventure.

Tip #91: Packing What You Want vs. What You Need.
People tend to over pack. Those "might use" items often are rarely used. Keep in mind that almost anything you need can be

purchased onboard or in ports of call. This makes packing less worrisome. Stick to a checklist as you pack, so as not to take an excessive number of items.

Tip #92: Pre-Pack Your Bags a Week Early.
This cruise hack takes a lot of last minute pressure off your shoulders. Pre-packing your cruise vacation bags early provides you some distinct benefits, namely:

1. You'll know how many items you can actually pack, which is reassuring.
2. You won't be scrambling last minute to wash or track down items.
3. You'll have time to pick up items you intend on taking, yet still need to purchase.
4. You'll psychologically be more relaxed as your cruise vacation approaches.

Tip #93: Where to Pack Your Liquids.
Should you decide to take any liquids in your carry-on bag, then you're limited to containers no larger than 3.25 ounces. All of these bottles must fit within one 1-quart, clear plastic bag. Perhaps the easier route to go is to place your liquids within your checked luggage. In which case, you can pack any size container that you desire. You want to avoid feeling like a very small nun at a penguin hunt when going through airport security.

Tip #94: Rolling Along.
In order to minimize creases and wrinkles appearing in your skirts and pants, roll rather than fold these clothing items. Ideally, you'll want to group like items together in separate bags or a travel packing system. This makes it convenient to unpack and find items.

Tip #95: Roll and Stuff.
Want to save space? Try rolling your socks and underwear and stick them snuggly in your shoes. This not only saves space, but also keeps the shape of your shoes intact. You could also place the clothing items in a small plastic bag before stuffing to keep them fresher. If you know what I mean.

Tip #96: The Eagle Has Landed.
Eagle Creek has an extensive list of lightweight, nylon packing systems designed with the traveler in mind. Placing your rolled clothing items in these well-designed bags, not only keeps like items together but also saves space. We've eliminated a 2nd piece of luggage by using these efficient packing systems. The best thing about the bags is that they quickly allow you to unpack your items from your suitcase and place them in the cabin's drawers or on shelves.

Tip #97: Bag It and Take It Home.
Pack a laundry bag. This could be as simple as a couple of large plastic bags or commercially-made bags like Eagle Creek's that are designed for separating dirty or damp laundry from clean clothes. Although most cruise ships have laundry facilities on-board, you may not want to spend your precious time doing it. Heck! You're on vacation, right?

Tip #98: Keep Your Clean Clothes Clean.
When packing your luggage either for going to or coming from your cruise, place any dirty footwear in either small plastic bags or use a zipped nylon bag designed for transporting shoes. In a pinch, you could use a couple of disposable shower caps for your dirtiest pair of shoes.

Tip #99: Wanna Hang out with Me?

There never seems to be enough hangers in cruise cabins or hotel rooms for that matter. Pack a few lightweight plastic hangers to help keep clothing items wrinkle free. We usually take a couple of regular hangers, along with a couple designed for pants.

Tip #100: Ask for Hangars.

An alternative to packing portable hangars is to ask your cabin steward to bring you a few extras as soon as you board. Doing so early, more than likely means that your request will be honored.

Tip #101: Ah! The Infamous Patty Stacker.

You'll be amazed at how much a lightweight, collapsible, door-hanging shoe rack can hold. Just hang it up on your cupboard door for additional storage space for any small items - and not just your shoes. Going vertical with your storage needs frees up space on counters and desks.

Tip #102: You Pegged It Right.

Most cruise ship cabins have a retractable clothesline in the bathtub. Bring along some clothes pegs to help hold up wet bathing suits or hand-washed items. You can also use them when drying your clothes on your balcony chairs, should you have a balcony suite. The pegs will give you some peace of mind that your clothes won't fly away in the wind and end up on some deserted island. You can also use the clothes pegs to hold drapes or curtains shut should the light be streaming into your cabin - unless you have an inside room.

Tip #103: Smelling Like a Rose.

Placing a scented dryer sheet in your luggage helps to keep everything smelling fresh. Just ensure that you don't place it near any perishable or open food items as it will taint them.

Tip #104: Fragile! Handle with Care.

We've come across this somewhat dubious cruise hack before. Placing a "Fragile" sticker on your checked luggage gives the appearance that your bag should be handled with kid gloves. Fragile items are usually packed last on airplanes and off-loaded first, which may speed up your travel connections.

Tip #105: All Packed? Smile for the Camera.

Take a photo of your luggage with your smartphone or tablet before you leave on your vacation. Should your luggage get lost in transit, having a photo of it helps the airline or cruise line look for the items. You'll be readily able to describe the lost item by having a visual reference.

Tip #106: Traveling with Disney?

If you would like to free up some luggage space when getting ready for your cruise, consider shipping baby supplies to the cruise port. With Disney, you can have items shipped up to 2 weeks ahead of time. Once the items arrive at your departure port, they'll deliver them to your cabin for you.

7

YOUR PERSONAL ID, PAPERS AND MONEY

Getting your paperwork in order for your cruise can be confusing. We've taken the mystery out of what to take and why with the following cruise hacks.

Tip #107: Hey, Good Looking!
Have at least 2 forms of government issued picture ID, such as a Passport and Driver's License. Some cruise lines and Ports of Call require that you take along photo ID for shore excursions. You may feel uncomfortable bringing your passport along if you're at the beach, so grab your driver's license instead. It's much easier to replace than your passport.

Since most cruises involve international travel, make arrangements to have a current passport as soon as possible. It should be valid at least six months beyond the scheduled date of travel. Keep in mind that any time you fly internationally you'll require a valid passport. So, should you have to fly from an international port of call for whatever reason, your driver's license won't cut the mustard.

Tip #108: I'm Not a Terrorist.

My wife Cindy was held up at debarkation because her name popped up on an Interpol hit list. No, she's not a known international gun for hire. Fortunately, she was able to prove her identity since she had emailed all of her important documents to herself.

We have gotten into the habit of creating PDF file documents such as birth certificates, passports, driver's licenses, government issued ID, important contact numbers, travel plans and reservations. Quick access to these files via your email account, makes it easier to handle any unforeseen issues.

Tip #109: Have a Backup Plan.

This tip piggybacks off the previous one. Have photocopies of your essential travel documents packed separately from your originals. We keep our original documents on our person or with our carry-on luggage, with the backup copies in our checked luggage. We like to neatly organize them together in clear document folders.

Make at least three copies of the fronts and backs of your most important documents, such as your passport, driver's license, insurance cards, prescriptions, airline tickets, hotel reservations, car rentals, emergency contact numbers and the like. Keep one copy in your carry-on bag and a second copy either in a second carry-on bag or in your checked luggage. Leave one copy with family back at home. Once onboard ship, place one copy of your photocopied documents in your cruise safe. Keep the other copy with you in your onshore bag. Now you've got your bases covered in the event of an emergency.

Tip #110: Show Me the Money Honey.

Major credit cards are accepted at most shops and restaurants at

Ports of Call. However, they may not be accepted at the local markets or locations outside the cruise terminal's catchment area. This is why we arrange to have a small stash of foreign currency with us before we travel.

We take one and five dollar bills in whatever currency is the main currency of our destination with us. Most popular travel destinations take the American dollar. If not, and you're strapped for cash, you'll usually find a currency exchange desk onboard your ship or one at the Port of Call. However, to get the best exchange rates, check at home with your local financial institution prior to your cruise vacation.

Tip #111: Tipping Porters, Cab Drivers, Bus Drivers, Waiters, etc.
Pre-plan for tips by taking a stack of $1, $5, $10 and $20 bills. A buck or two a bag is a common practice for baggage handlers. If you're traveling to poorer or less stable countries, tipping becomes an important practice. You don't want to have to report your lost or damaged luggage because you chose not to tip. A few dollars here and there won't hurt you. Small bills are handy when tipping stewards, tour guides or waiters when in port.

Tip #112: Convenience Comes with a Price.
ATMs aboard most cruise ships dispense cash in U.S. dollars. Using them may cost you a hefty fee, which could be up to $5 in addition to what your bank charges you. Using a debit card from a bank that reimburses ATM fees, is a great way to save a few bucks. If no ATM is available, see if you can use your credit card to draw cash in the ship's casino or at the purser's desk. Of course, the best course of action is to anticipate how much you might need for cash expenses while cruising and bring that with you from home.

Tip #113: Foreign Travel to Europe or Asia?
Traveler's checks can be a good means of accessing cash because if they're stolen or lost, they can easily be replaced. Keep a note of the serial numbers of each check separately from the actual checks themselves. If you do lose the checks or they get stolen, this record of serial numbers can help the bank trace the checks and issue replacements much faster. Many European and Asian cruise lines will cash traveler's checks at the purser's desk. Go online or contact your cruise line directly to get the specifics as to what check-cashing services are provided.

Tip #114: Hey Big Boy! What's that Lump?
Invest in an under-garment money pouch. These discreet travel pouches are designed to hold a few bills and some ID under your clothing out of sight. Pickpocketing can be an issue in some tourist destinations. Being proactive by placing your valuables in a safe location as you explore your Ports of Call eliminates yet another worry. It beats trying to hide your money in a shoe, right?

Tip #115: Need Foreign Currency?
As previously mentioned, foreign currency exchange rates onboard ship or in ports of call tend to be pricey. Your best bet is to get the foreign currencies before you depart on your cruise and top-up at your destinations if you don't have enough. Fortunately, most of the popular ports of call in the Caribbean and Mexico gladly accept the American greenback.

Tip #116: Strapped for Cash? Option 1.
To avoid paying the high fees charged by ATM's located onboard your ship, head over to the casino instead. You can usually use your card to extract U.S. cash for little or no cost.

Tip #117: Strapped for Cash? Option 2.

Should you have onboard credits assigned to your account use a similar tactic. Convert that credit to cash by using your sail card to deposit money into a casino's slot machine. Rather than gamble this money away, withdraw the credit as a voucher and have the purser turn it into cash.

Tip #118: Do You Have Scuba Certification or Handicapped Parking ID?

Don't forget to pack your scuba certificate should you be planning to do some dives at any of your ports of call. And should you have a handicapped parking sticker, photocopy several color copies that you can pull out in a pinch if needed.

8

WHAT TO WEAR?

Most first-time cruisers end up packing too much. And often many of these items aren't needed or used. We'll show you a number of simple strategies as to how to select your clothing items with the following cruise hacks.

Tip #119: How Much Clothing Will Be Enough?

For a seven-day cruise pack no more than three or four standard outfits for day-to-day use, plus one formal (business casual) outfit. You'll also want a half dozen sets of underwear and socks. This will give you enough of the basics from which to build your cruise wardrobe. Sound good?

Tip #120: Making the Most of What You've Packed.

Hanging up and airing out your shirts, dresses, skirts and pants after you use them, should help to extend the life out of your garments over the course of a week. Some cruise ships even have self-laundry facilities or you could bring some detergent from home to hand wash items in a pinch.

Tip #121: Pack in Terms of Outfits.
Rather than just throw a bunch of your favorite tops and bottom together, think about packing a "set" of clothes for each of the following types of activities:

- Beach/ poolside wear.
- Dining room and nightlife wear (semi-formal).
- Formal wear or business casual attire (usually worn twice on a 7-day cruise).
- Active or sport wear (for the gym, spa, sports, ports of call).
- Inclement weather gear (rainwear, warm jackets and accessories).

Tip #122: Pack in Terms of Layers.
This piggybacks off of the previous tip. Pack color-coordinated items that can be layered on as the weather changes. You'll not only save space, but also be styling. Wouldn't that be awesome?

Tip #123: Take Two! Ready! Action!
Take two bathing suits. There's nothing worse than putting on a cold, clammy, wet suit. Yikes! I cringe at the thought. When you're cruising, lots of onboard activities revolve around a water theme. You may end up spending the majority of your time in your swim attire. Also take suits that'll allow you to participate in water sports or more physical activities than just lounging around. If you're like me, you'll see me hitting Mach 1 on the water slide with all the other 10-year olds. Having a form-fitting suit avoids the "wedgie" effect." If you know what I mean.

Tip #124: I'm Freezing My Yichees Off!
Despite you being in a tropical paradise, evenings and early mornings can be chilly. Pack a lightweight, insulated jacket or

sweater for cool or windy nights on deck. I like to pack a compressible, insulated jacket that I can also take with me on excursions should the need arise.

Tip #125: Burn Baby Burn!
Invest in a rash guard, long-sleeved shirt to protect you from the sun and chafing. You'll be glad you did, especially if you're planning on doing any water-related activities when in port. Look for quick-drying shirts that offer an SFP rating of 30 or higher. Be aware that some excursions prohibit you from using sun screens or perfumed products, like visiting the underground caves of The Secret River in Cozumel, which we highly recommend.

Tip #126: Be Like Jesse James.
Take a wide brimmed hat, along with a neckerchief or Buff. It's important to protect yourself from the sun, wouldn't you agree? Tilley hats are a great option. Designed by a sailor, these stylish hats offer great protection from the sun. And they float, to boot.

A Buff is another great accessory, especially if you're a Survivor fan. It can be used in various ways, such as a tank top, sun hat, dust protector, sweatband, hair tie or even as a facecloth.

Tip #127: Keep Those Feet Cool.
Ensure that you pack waterproof flip-flops or sandals for hanging out by the pool or beach. They won't be well-suited for a hike through the jungle. However, they're a great lightweight deck shoe when onboard.

Tip #128: Treat Your Puppies Well.
Comfy walking shoes are great for exploring and sight-seeing during port of calls. A cushioned, supportive shoe should even allow you to enjoy more remote locations where there might be

some wonderful hiking trails. Those sexy sandals probably look great. However, after a day of exploring, you'll wish you were wearing a more comfortable alternative. Or, wishing you were back on ship resting those tired puppies while sipping on your favorite foo-foo drink.

Tip #129: You Look Ravishing Darling.

Typically, on a week-long cruise, you'll have the opportunity to dress to the nines. There'll be evenings where you'll be encouraged to dress up in formal wear. You'll find that many cruisers tend to go all out on these nights. So, if you don't want to feel left out, bring some fancy, dress clothes and join in the fun. At a minimum, pack at least something that is suitable for "business casual" so that you won't be rejected at the main dining room or at any of the upscale specialty restaurants.

Tip #130: Avoid Those 6" Stilettoes.

They may look sexy; but do you really want to be wearing a cast? Don't forget that cruise ships are at the mercy of ocean waves. It's challenging enough to walk with those puppies on dry land. Unless you like walking around looking like a drunk chicken or enjoy tripping over your own feet, opt for a flatter-soled shoe.

Tip #131: This Straw Didn't Break the Camel's Back.

Concerned about arriving on ship with a tangled mess of necklaces? Try threading each necklace through a straw and then fasten the clasp. You'll end up with a fully stretched, untangled necklace. Voila!

Tip #132: Button, Button Who's Got the Button.

This cruise hack piggybacks off of the previous one. Earrings can also become a tangled mess when traveling. To avoid this scenario,

put each pair of earrings through a button and fasten the clasps.
Now you have a simple, hassle-free way of grabbing your earrings.

Tip #133: Enjoy Your Excursions even MORE!

If you're going to be physically active on your cruise, then your
sport clothing needs to be both comfortable and functional. You'll
benefit from bringing appropriate clothing for certain activities,
such as:

- Cycling: padded cycling shorts & gloves.
- Kayaking: rash guard shirt, neoprene water shoes or
  form-fitting sandals.
- Water slide: form-fitting bathing suit. Opt for a one-piece
  suit rather than a bikini. If you catch my drift (or your suit
  may).
- Snorkeling: face mask & especially your own snorkel.

Tip #134: Forget about Drying off by Rolling in the Sand.

We always pack a lightweight, quick drying, microfiber
"**PackTowl**" towel for Ports of Call. Should you be looking into
investing in one of these absorbent towels, save yourself some
money, buy an extra-large, "original" towel and cut it in half giving
you 2 towels. If they initially feel stiff to the touch, wash them
before packing. We take our towels on vacation everywhere.

Tip #135: Get Ready to Party.

All cruise ships will have a few theme nights whether it be a
formal black-tie dinner or a costume party. These theme nights
are more enjoyable when you're dressed appropriately as it makes
you feel more involved. Check online as to what the themes are
beforehand so you can prepare your outfit. Some seasoned
cruisers go a long way into creating custom-made outfits.

Tip #136: Stop the Shivering and Teeth Chattering.
Even though you may be heading to the warm waters of the
Caribbean, being able to stay in the water for long periods of time
may be a challenge. We like to throw on a lightweight neoprene
vest and/or shorts for water activities at Ports of Call. Keeping your
core warm enables you to spend more time in the water, especially
if you're on an excursion swimming in a cenote or snorkeling
along a coral reef.

Tip #137: Hey! Where Did My Flip Flop Drift Off Too?
When in port, take water shoes that actually stay on your feet and
provide some protection against abrasion. If possible, avoid
relying solely on flip flops when out on excursions. The crystal
blue waters at the beach are enticing. However, the coral below the
surface can really slice up the sides of your feet when you don't
have adequate protection.

Tip #138: Are You Leaving from the Arctic for a Caribbean Vacation?
If so, then leave that down winter parka back home in your closet
or igloo. Yes, it may be -30 outside and you might be tempted to
pack warm winter gear to get you to the airport. There is a better
alternative. Instead of that bulky parka, use a layered approach.
Take along a warm sweater and insulated synthetic (not down)
windproof, water resistant jacket. Having worked for The North
face, we like to take along a lightweight, compressible layer like a
Thermoball jacket. The insulated jacket can be worn on ship
when the nights are cool or when its windy. Much more practical,
wouldn't you agree?

Tip #139: I Love Convertibles.
Since most of my cruising is done in the Caribbean, I've invested
in pants that convert into shorts. The weather can change abruptly
when traveling from being overheated as the day unfolds to cold

and miserable when the wind picks up. Being able to zip off my pant bottoms when the afternoon sun heats things up, makes my excursions that much more comfortable. Not to mention that convertible pants can save you packing space. Now, we're cruising in style!

Tip #140: Arrive with Your Dress Shirt Collars Intact.
Dress shirt collars can really get mangled when traveling. To keep your collars intact and crisp looking, thread a belt around the collar as you would a necktie. Then, cinch it up tightly so that the weight of other items won't cause the collar to collapse under pressure. Of course, this hack won't work if your pants keep slipping down to your knees when travelling to your cruise. Then again, you could always pack a second belt, right?

9

TRAVELING WITH CHILDREN

Providing your children with a safe, fun experience is the focus of this chapter. Just a handful of these tips will give you a greater sense of peace of mind knowing that you'll be able to better address some common challenges.

Tip #141: Pack for the Pool.
Ensure that your children have packed their swim attire and active ware in their carry-on luggage. They'll be as excited as clams at high tide once you board the ship. In all likelihood, they'll high tail it to the pool deck. Checked luggage may not arrive at your cabin until much later in the evening. Don't miss out having to wait for your bags to arrive.

Tip #142: Disposable Bibs Save on Laundry.
If you're taking babies and young toddlers on a cruise with you, use paper bibs that you can simply throw away after each meal. This enable you to protect their clothes from any mess. You also don't have to cart a dirty, stained bib around with you - unless you really want to.

Tip #143: Strolling Along.
This tip may be a no-brainer. When you need to keep your young child safe or if they're tired use a stroller. A foldable stroller is an ideal way of doing this. Most cruises accommodate the transportation of strollers. Just ensure that the unit you take will be lightweight and compact enough to fit in your cabin and move about the ship.

Tip #144: Rein Them In.
Hyperactive rug rats can sprint off at the blink of an eye. If your toddler has a tendency to be an explorer like Indiana Jones, reins may be a great option. Reins allow them to explore their surroundings, yet be under parental control - assuming you're holding the other end.

Tip #145: Child Proof Your Room.
Bring along a roll of tape that you can use to secure drawers and cupboards. The tape can also be used to securely hold a washcloth or other soft material on sharp cornered objects like desks and tables. More on tape later.

Tip #146: Dinner Pampering for Kids.
Should you be traveling with a cruise line like Disney, consider opting into their "dine and play" program. At the second dinner seating, children between 3 and 12 will get priority service and then be taken to a separate play area. This allows you and your spouse some quality time to enjoy your dinner.

Tip #147: Pack Familiar Snacks.
Minimize those temper tantrums, by bringing some of your children's favorite snacks. Kids can be picky eaters at times. Unfamiliar food and surroundings may have your child balking at eating anything simply because it's unfamiliar and strange to

them. For these tough situations pack some comfort food. You'll also save some money bringing your own, especially in airports and ports of call where purchasing these items can be on the pricey side.

Tip #148: The Comforts of Home.
This is a no-brainer. Ensure you bring enough "baby/ toddler" supplies to last you the trip, plus a little extra. Most ships sell items at a premium, but don't count on them having your favorite brand. Do some advance planning by creating a packing checklist specific to meeting the needs of your infant.

Tip #149: Forget Something? No worries.
Most cruise ships can provide you with what you need when taking care of little ones. Whether it be baby food or cribs, you just need to ask. A word of advice. The earlier you make your requests the easier it may be to honor them. You may not be the only family needing items.

Tip #150: Program's for Toddlers.
Traveling with toddlers? Carnival is one of the few cruise lines that has a children's program for 2-year old toddlers. Most Kid Club programs on other cruise lines start at three years old. Verify prior to booking if this is the case. It may sway or influence your decision as to which cruise ship to book.

Tip #151: Enroll in Free Daycare.
Most cruise ships have professionally staffed daycare centers that provide a plethora of activities such as crafts, sports, and movies. This frees up your time to relax and enjoy activities on your own. If you have kids, make full use of this popular child care service. These daytime services are included in the price of the ticket so you may as well make full use of it. Wouldn't you agree?

10

BEVERAGES

Many cruisers would like to bring certain beverages along with them on the cruise in an attempt to save money and to drink what they enjoy. The following cruise hacks address the most common questions as to how to go about bringing those items onboard.

Tip #152: You're Not a Camel.
We've taken both plastic water bottles and hydration systems on our cruises in the past. Having access to fresh, cold water when in port or out on an excursion keeps you from getting dehydrated or sick. Nowadays, we always take a lightweight 32-L backpack equipped with a 2-L Camelback hydration system on our excursions. Similarly, water bottles are great for keeping juice or pop in your room or walking about on deck. You can easily refill your bottle in any of the main dining areas. A water bottle is also a discreet way of drinking other beverages - if you know what I mean.

Tip #153: Particular about Water Quality?
Look into bringing your own bottled water to save money. Most

cruise lines allow you to bring a limited quantity of non-alcoholic beverages onboard. Check with your particular cruise line as to what types of beverages and quantities are allowed.

Tip #154: *Know Thy Limit.*
You're usually allowed 1 bottle of wine per guest. We typically pack one bottle each in our carry-on bags for easy inspection. Also, don't forget a corkscrew. And don't forget to pack it in your checked luggage if you're flying in from your home town to the cruise port. Otherwise, you may have to forfeit it at airport security. The most restrictive cruise lines for bringing alcohol onboard are MSC Cruise, Costa and Royal Caribbean. And the more lenient major players are Carnival, Disney, Holland America, Norwegian, Princess and Celebrity.

Tip #155: *Protect Your Wine Bottles.*
A neoprene, protective sleeve or plastic bubble wrap designed for bottles does a great job of preventing any unwelcome surprises when you unpack your wine bottle. In a pinch, you could also place the neck of your bottle in a pair of shoes. The neck is the most vulnerable part of the bottle when traveling.

Tip #156: *Will They Notice that I Snuck Alcohol on Board?*
Maybe, maybe not. While frowned upon by the cruise industry, many seasoned cruisers do it indiscreetly. It depends on how you pack your checked luggage. Consider taking your favorite alcohol in irregular-shaped collapsible plastic bottles. They're less likely to show up on the X-ray screens. But, you do need to factor in the consequences should you get caught, which could be as drastic as not being allowed on the ship at embarkation.

Tip #157: *Into Wacky Weed?*
Smoking drugs is not tolerated on cruises. Period. However, for

those seeking the medicinal benefits that cannabis has to offer, consider taking a vaporizer like the "Crafty" along with a "Smoke Buddy" hand-held portable carbon filter. Vaping into a carbon filter eliminates most of the odors. As an alternative, bring along some canna-caps or your favorite edibles, which are more discreet.

11

MISCELLANEOUS ITEMS

What simple items could make your cruise that much more enjoyable? We'll be sharing a myriad of cruise hacks that'll allow you to enjoy being pampered even more. Not everything mentioned will resonate with you, nor should you pack everything mentioned. Select those tips that make the most sense to you in helping you create a memorable experience with fewer hassles or challenges.

Tip #158: What about Ouwie Boo Boo's?
A small, simple first aid kit is a good thing to have with you when you leave the ship. At a minimum, pack a few waterproof bandages, some wet wipes and a travel-size bottle of sanitary hand wash for when you're unable to get to a sink. Fortunately, there is always a first aide responder available on the ship in case of an emergency or illness, but you should be prepared anyways.

Tip #159: Is the Boogie Man Coming? It's Dark in Here.
Pack a portable, compact headlight and/or nightlight for emergencies, such as getting up in the middle of the night to pee.

You don't want to wake up the rest of the cabin by flipping on the light switch, right? Also, a portable light source can be helpful if you're in an interior cabin. You'll find interior cabins to be almost pitch black with the lights turned off and this can be pretty scary for youngsters.

Tip #160: Did Something Die in Here?

After spending a few days in an inside cabin, you may be asking yourself this question. Cabins can get pretty stuffy after a few days of being at the beach, hanging out poolside or working out in the fitness facility. Consider bringing along an air freshener or some Febreeze or Ozium spray to help control those musty odors.

Tip #161: Getting into Hot Water.

Bring an insulated water flask with you on your cruise if you would like immediate access to hot water. Just fill it up when you're in the dining area and take it back to your room. Since kettles are prohibited on cruise ships, you'll need to get hot water from the dining area or order it through room service. Few cruise lines provide insulated hot water containers. And room service may not be convenient or timely for you, especially if you're having to deal with baby formula.

Tip #162: Caffeine Addict?

Ah coffee! That sweet balm by which we shall accomplish tasks. If you're like me, having a bountiful supply of coffee in the morning helps me get revved up for the day's activities. I like to wander around the deck in the morning. Having an insulated, no-spill coffee mug with me makes my morning ritual that much more enjoyable. Consider packing your favorite no-spill mug if you enjoy this dark nectar of the God's as much as I do.

Tip #163: What to Do with Travel Medication.
For ease of use, pack your daily medication and vitamins in a 7-day medicine container. Although the airlines prefer seeing your meds in their original bottles, placing your daily allotment into a week-long plastic storage container makes life easier. Also, keep your supply of essential meds with you in your carry-on bag. Pack a few extras in your checked luggage in case your departure home is delayed.

Tip #164: Prone to Motion Sickness?
Although cruise ships are designed to be very stable, ship motion cannot be totally eliminated especially during choppy seas. If you're prone to seasickness, consult your pharmacist or doctor about medications to take in case of motion sickness. Do this prior to your cruise, as you may find a limited selection of medication onboard. Two of the most common medications are Dramamine II tablets and Scopolamine patches.

Tip #165: Pack an Extra Pill Box.
Rather than bring your heavy, mahogany jewelry case with you, consider packing the jewelry you'll need in a daily pill box. This'll keep your earrings, necklaces and rings organized in a central location, which is also inconspicuous and safe.

Tip #166: Supplement Your Digestion.
Many of us take vitamin, mineral and digestive supplements when we're at home. Should you fall into this category, don't forget to pack a supply with you. We suggest taking a probiotic to help regulate your digestion while onboard and traveling. When you're eating 5 or 6 square meals a day of all sorts of ethnic cuisine, you're bound to need some help in the digestion department. If you're currently not taking a probiotic, introduce one a week or so before your trip so as to better acclimate your digestive system.

Tip #167: Avoid Leaky Messes.
Bottles can be notorious for springing a leak in the worst possible spot in your luggage. Try placing small squares of plastic wrap over the mouth of each bottle, before screwing on the top. This'll help to seal the bottle once it's tightly shut.

Tip #168: Be Wrinkle Free.
Travel irons are not permitted on most cruise lines. So how do you look your best and keep your clothes wrinkle free when cruising? A simple solution is to pack a travel-size bottle of a wrinkle releaser spray. Not only does the spray help to minimize wrinkling, it also cuts down on odors and smells divine. Well, maybe not divine.

Tip #169: Wrinkle Free the Natural way.
An alternative to using a commercial wrinkle spray, is to run the hot water in your shower for a couple of minutes. Then, hang your wrinkled items in the steamy environment. After a few minutes pull out your items and hand stretch them to remove most of the creases.

Tip #170: Don't Forget Your Lucky Bingo Marker.
With bingo being a popular onboard activity, why not pack your favorite, lucky marker. Yet, another simple overlooked item that'll help to kick up your cruise experience a notch.

Tip #171: Become a Captain High-Lighter.
Every evening the next day's onboard activities will be printed and delivered to your cabin. Use a couple of colored highlighters to mark out your plans on your daily guide so you don't miss anything. This is an easy way to identify activities that you would like to participate in while onboard.

Tip #172: Stick to It to Stay in Touch.
Sticky notes are an easy way of communicating with both crew members and family or friends. These colorful notes can alert your cabin steward as to special requests like ice, extra pillows or blankets etc. Just place them on a mirror where there're easily spotted. It's also a nice touch just to let your cabin steward know that they're appreciated. Traveling with friends or family? Use these notes to let your travel companions know where you are or where to meet later that day. They're easy to recognize when placed on a door or a table - not so much when placed in an empty wine bottle and set adrift in the sea.

Tip #173: Door Decorations. Cool!
It's amazing how every cabin door looks identical when walking down a hallway. You may even walk right past your cabin, like we have. And we're supposed to be experienced cruisers! Consider bringing along a simple decoration like a balloon, poster, streamer, or even a Post It note to make your room easier to find.

Tip #174: Dry Erase Board.
A small dry erase board placed on or beside your cabin door is a great way to stay in touch with friends and family. Simply leave a note on the board for others to see. This way others will know where to find you or what their plans might be. The board also makes it easier to locate your cabin as you're walking down the hallway.

Tip #175: Bring or Purchase a Souvenir Lanyard.
A neck lanyard is a convenient way to hold your Cruise ID. Upon embarkation, cruise guests are given a credit-card size card that acts as a room key, onboard credit card and identification for coming and going on the cruise ship. Wearing a lanyard keeps your ID safe around your neck and easily accessible.

Tip #176: Magnetic Hooks? Genius!

Most cabin walls are metal and as such can support a magnetic hook. Magnetic hooks are a convenient way of hanging up your cruise lanyard, a bathing suit, your hat or other lightweight item that you might be using on a regular basis. This'll help to reduce any clutter around your cabin.

Tip #177: Pack a Long Rope and/or Bungie Cord.

No, this is not to tie up your kids with when they misbehave. If you have a balcony, a rope or cord will keep your door open by tying the door handle to a railing or heavy furniture. Yes, the balcony cabins are climate controlled. However, you may enjoy the smell of fresh sea air in the morning or at sunset.

Tip #178: Take the Right Sunscreen.

In 2021, Hawaii's ban on sunscreens containing octinoxate and oxybenzone also known as BP-3 takes effect. These chemical compounds have been linked to coral reef destruction. Mineral sunscreens that use zinc oxide or titanium dioxide to physically block the sun's rays will still be allowed. Be aware that this trend may extend to other endangered coral reefs in the world. Sunscreen is a very important item to have. Consider taking along a SPF 30 or higher, broad spectrum, water-resistant sunscreen.

Tip #179: Duct Tape Sandals, My Dear?

Duct tape has versatile applications from repairing tears in rain shells to securing travel bags with broken zippers shut. I've even seen creative individuals fashion a pair of duct tape slippers for cabin use. Go figure!

Tip #180: Let's See. Did I Pack My Glasses?

Don't forget to take a spare set of eye glasses or contacts, along with a pair of sun glasses. If you're visually challenged like me, you don't want to miss out on seeing spectacular events unfolding before your eyes should you have lost or misplaced your original pair.

Tip #181: Everything Is So Foggy.
Piggybacking off the previous tip, pack a small, travel-size bottle of eyeglass cleaner. Sunscreen and oils can quickly cloud your lenses. Having a cleaner handy, gives you a whole new perspective of what's out on the horizon. By selecting the right cleaner, you could even use it to keep your camera lenses and filters crystal clear.

Tip #182: Crap! I Can't See that Far.
Pack along a pair of binoculars or opera glasses for those great sightseeing moments. More often than not, cruise lines take you to scenic places. You'll appreciate having a pair of binoculars with you when whale or porpoise watching.

Tip #183: It's Bigger than a Beach Towel.
You could always pack your favorite beach towel for lying out on a sandy beach when at a port of call. Or, you can grab an inexpensive bed sheet from home and use that instead. The bed sheet will probably take up less room in your luggage and provide you with a larger surface area to lie on when soaking up the sun.

Tip #184: Pack a Travel Umbrella.
Having a travel umbrella on shore excursions has a dual purpose. Should a shower develop, you've got some protection from the rain. And even if there is no forecast of rain, take one along. The umbrella offers protection from the direct rays of the sun. You don't want to return to the ship looking like a freshly picked tomato, do you?

Tip #185: Bored or Having to Wait?

Pack your favorite board or card game. We love to play the board game "Labyrinth" when we're waiting around for our next planned activity to start. We just place all of the board pieces and cards in a large Zip-lock plastic bag and tuck the board into our checked luggage. We've also taken board games like "Blokus", "Yahtzee" and "Scrabble" along depending on our mood.

Tip #186: The Light Switch Hack.

Many cruise lines require that you use your sail card to activate the light switch in your room by the door. To get around this inconvenience, try using another credit-card size card, such as an old store membership card.

Tip #187: Are You a Light Sleeper?

Take along a few pairs of disposable ear plugs. Cruise ships are noisier than your typical house. The sounds of the ship, noisy cabin neighbors, or even loud music can be an unwelcome distraction. Ear plugs will help to muffle the sound.

Tip #188: What's that Noise?

A compact, portable white noise machine may help you and your cabin mates sleep better. There are many compact models to choose from. If you're traveling with infants, this may be a great way to quickly send them off to La-La land.

Tip #189: Stay Cooler. Fans Welcome.

Adjusting the air conditioning in your cabin may be challenging. Rather than resorting to sleeping stark naked to stay cool should your cabin temperature be an issue, consider bringing along a small, portable fan. You may even find that the fan's white noise helps you sleep better.

Tip #190: Where Can I Wash My hands?

An overlooked item to pack is either a travel-size bottle of hand sanitizer or pre-packaged wet towels. They're convenient when you need a quick wipe. These items are very practical when you're on a shore excursion since many facilities can be pretty primitive.

Tip #191: On the Cutting Edge.

Should you not have a storage container designed specifically to hold your razor, here's an alternative strategy. Place a wide, binder clip over the head of your razor. This keeps it from damaging other items in your toiletries kit, not to mention your fingers as well.

Tip #192: Don't Be a Pack Rat.

No need to pack everything you think you might need, plus the kitchen sink just in case. You can leave your blow dryer, clothes iron and even your bath robe at home. Also, you'll want to limit your sundries like soap & shampoo as these items come standard fare in your cabin.

12

TAKING ALONG ELECTRONICS

Cruising presents some unique challenges when trying to keep all of your electronic devices up and running. These cruise hacks focus on just that, being able to optimize the use of your devices and what you should consider packing.

Tip #193: Captain! The Di-lithium Crystals Are Failing.
When you're traveling with multiple electronic devices like smartphones, tablets, digital cameras, video cameras and the like, consolidating your adapters and chargers into one bag keeps things readily accessible and easy to find. Most cruise ship cabins have just a couple of power outlets available, which may not provide you with enough charging stations. Packing a lightweight, power board with 4 to 6 sockets will help keep your devices all charged up. Since some cruise lines don't allow surge protectors, place all of your charging devices and cords in your carry-on luggage so that your bag isn't delayed at embarkation because it has to be searched. We like to pack a compact Belkin multi-outlet and USB device.

Tip #194: The Power of a Tablet.
A tablet is a great multi-function device to take along on any
cruise. Even if you have no intention of connecting to the Internet
you can use these devices as an eBook reader, for taking photos, to
play games, for watching videos or to document your adventures.
You'll also benefit from connecting to the on-board Wi-Fi to access
the free content on your cruise ship. You'll be able to find out
about the ship and its facilities, along with the current day's
activity plan.

Tip #195: I'm All Tangled Up!
Earphones, USB cords, and chargers can become a tangled mess
when traveling. Should you have a spare eyeglass or sunglass
container, neatly place your cords in the container so that you
don't end up with a ball to unravel.

Tip #196: Are You an Avid Reader?
Don't forget to pack your favorite reads. Rather than take bulky
books along with you, we suggest that you use a device like a
Kindle reader. A Kindle reading device is easier to use when out
on the deck, especially when the sun is shining. You'll find that
these devices have less glare than most tablets. You'll also be able
to use it another way, which will be revealed in tip #279.

Tip #197: Strapped for Power Sources?
Most modern TVs have USB slots which you can use for charging
devices like smartphones and tablets. Should charging all of your
devices be a challenge, check out the back of your TV to see if you
have a USB slot that you can tap into.

Tip #198: Roger Wilco. 10-4 Big Buddy.
Large group? Stay connected with walkie-talkies, rather than
trying to text on your phone. Mobile devices are not a practical

means of staying in touch with your party when you're in the middle of the ocean. If you intend on buying a set of walkie-talkies, just ensure that your devices are capable of covering the entire ship. Opt for the more powerful 5-watt radios, which should give you 800 to 1000 feet of reception on your floating tin can. All that metal will affect reception of the radio signals, so it's better to use devices that can handle the interference.

Tip #199: Capture Memories.

We find that the most precious aspect of our cruises is capturing memories. We always pack a digital camera, a GoPro video camera, an iPad and a cell phone with a selfie stick. This enable us to take both spontaneous photos and videos. Once back home, I'll convert all of the images into short video montages that can be viewed on a digital picture frame or even uploaded to our You Tube channel.

Tip #200: Why Invest in a GoPro?

A **GoPro** is a waterproof video camera that's ideal for capturing wonderful memories. It's compact, easy-to-use and won't miss a thing with its wide-angle lens. Water activities tend to be a central theme of all cruises. Having a waterproof camera on hand allows you to take incredible video clips around the pool, at the beach or an any water adventure.

Tip #201: Music to My Ears.

If you enjoy listening to music at home and want to re-create that ambiance, bring a wired or Bluetooth speaker that works off of your smartphone, iPod or tablet. Should you not be fussy about the sound quality, try placing your phone or iPod in a glass. This little trick will amplify the sound so that you can enjoy your favorite tunes while in your cabin.

13

YOUR PRE-CRUISE "TO DO" SCHEDULE

Simple planning and preparation are two essential ingredients to pulling off a memorable, worry-free cruise experience. These particular cruise hacks ensure that you're not faced with any surprises that could have been averted back home prior to your trip.

Tip #202: Put Your Credit Card on Vacation Alert.
Let your credit card company or debit card provider know that you'll be traveling. This can be done online for most card providers. By indicating when and where you'll be traveling, you won't have any unusual or embarrassing experiences should your card be declined due to suspicious activity.

Tip #203: Online Check-in.
Your cruise line will require that you check-in online and print off certain documents before you get to the cruise terminal. This speeds up the processing of the hundreds of passengers eager to get underway. You'll usually be expected to have baggage tags, your eTicket and health declaration forms printed prior to

embarkation. You should also confirm your bed configuration, dining preferences and special requests at this time.

Tip #204: Download the Cruise Ship's Mobile App.
Before you head out to sea, where roaming charges can be pricey, download the free mobile app to your smartphone. This'll connect you to onboard services, activity schedules, menus and the like.

Tip #205: Don't Be Disappointed. Book Online.
Pre-book excursions online with the cruise line or another provider before your cruise. Half the fun of going on a cruise is exploring the surrounding area when you're in port. Since many excursions have a limited capacity and can fill up quickly, pre-book those activities you plan on taking in. You don't want to waste your time standing in line the first or second day of your cruise twiddling your thumbs only to be told that the excursion is full when it's your turn in line.

Tip #206: Private Excursions with an Individual Experience.
ShoreFox.com is an online marketplace for private tours. The website can help you compare tour operators in more than 90 ports of call worldwide. This could save you up to 30% on a typical tour promoted by the cruise lines. Yet, another option for you to consider, right?

Tip #207: Celebrate in Style.
Are you celebrating a special occasion? Request an in-room surprise gift. You can coordinate this with your room steward or make arrangements online. Something as simple as a bottle of red wine and chocolates can go a long way in setting the tone and mood for your cruise.

Tip #208: Use an Exit Checklist.
Your departure day prior to embarking on your cruise can be a bit stressful and hectic. In the heat of the moment you may forget to do something. Having a checklist of those items you need to do prior to heading out the door will give you peace of mind. We like to go over a list that covers things like turning off lights, adjusting thermostats, checking the mail & garbage, powering down computers, turning off washing machines, etc. You get the picture.

Tip #209: Consider Registering Newly Acquired Items You'll Be Taking.
If you plan on taking expensive, relatively new items, such as computers or cameras, out of the country, think about registering them with Customs before you go. Having photocopies of sales receipts along with pictures of you holding the item in a location that is clearly within the country is also a good strategy to use to prove prior ownership.

Tip #210: Get Your Home Affairs in Order.
Make preliminary care arrangements for your home, yard and pets. You'll have a lot on your plate the last week prior to your cruise vacation. So, make arrangements a month out to give you enough time to address these important considerations.

Tip #211: Do Some Pre-Packing One Week Out.
As previously mentioned, by setting aside those items you know you'll be taking along with you, you'll be better prepared for your final packing day. This reduces the chances of leaving an essential item behind. And provides you with some comfort in knowing you've taken a proactive approach.

Tip #212: Periodically Check the Weather Reports.
A couple of days before you travel, check the weather reports for

potential weather delays for all destinations you'll be heading to. This becomes a more important consideration should you be flying during the winter months or across the country.

Tip #213: Confirm Your Flight.
Contact the airlines one day prior to departure to confirm your reservations. You'll avoid any unnecessary delays at the airport and potential mix-ups.

~

14

EMBARKATION DAY

What should you be doing on embarkation day? These cruise hacks focus on making the most of your first day and will help to maximize your time spent aboard.

Tip #214: The Early Bird Catches the Worm

Get onto your ship as early as you can, preferably about five hours before departure and at least two hours before the scheduled sailing. Arriving early gives you time to address any unforeseen problems, like forgetting documents back at the hotel. Cruise lines stagger arrivals so as to reduce waiting times. You'll be given a block of time in which you can board your ship. Try to arrive at least 30 minutes prior to your scheduled boarding time. This should place you near the front of the line. Once onboard you'll have more time to explore the ship before it gets insanely busy like the ant hill from the Indiana Jones movie The Crystal Skull.

Tip #215: Place Phones on Airplane Mode.

As soon as you arrive in port, switch your phone to airplane mode. You'll still be able to connect to the Internet via Wi-Fi. In all probability, your cruise will take you out of your service provider's network area. Should you opt to stay connected through your provider, you could end up paying hefty roaming charges.

Tip #216: *Pre-Print and Pre-Fill Any Embarkation Documents.*
To speed up processing and wait times, try to print off and complete the following documentation beforehand, if possible:

1. Boarding Pass.
2. Onboard Account papers.
3. Health Declaration forms.

As well, have both your passport and credit card ready for scanning. Once these documents have been processed, you'll be issued a sail card that serves as your room key, onboard charge card, and for documenting when you leave the ship at ports of call.

Tip #217: *What to Expect to Find in Your Cabin.*
Assume that your cabin will not be 100% ready when you arrive onboard. However, you can drop off your carry-on bags, change into more comfortable deck attire and head out to explore the ship. Your checked luggage may not arrive in your cabin until the supper hour. Yet, another reason why you should pack in your carry on what you need for making the most of the afternoon on deck.

Tip #218: *Get Acclimated Sooner than Later.*
Most guests will head up to the pool deck where they'll either grab a buffet lunch or take in the festivities around the pool deck. We like to do this as soon as possible before it gets too hectic. As well, after grabbing a bite to eat, we'll check out where all of the amenities onboard are located by going for a leisurely stroll.

Tip #219: Book Early or Be Disappointed.
If you didn't make online reservations prior to embarkation, do so in person as soon as possible once aboard. If you would like a spa/beauty treatment, special shore excursion, or specialty restaurant reservation, plan on getting this done early on the first afternoon. Most popular attractions and time slots fill up soon after embarkation.

Tip #220: Hiding Your Luggage.
Once you have unpacked your luggage, place your bags under your bed rather than in your closet. We like to unpack after we've had a bite to eat and explored the ship. This may be an obvious hack, but one that's overlooked by many first-time cruisers. The space under each bed is designed to accommodate your luggage. We also like to place our laundry in a bag that is tucked into one of the pieces of luggage. Out of sight; out of mind, right?

Tip #221: Extend the Life of Your Garments.
Once you receive all of your luggage, take a moment to hang up as many of your outfits as possible. Hanging up your clothing items airs them out, reduces creasing and extends the life of your items. You should be able to wear certain outfits more than once.

Tip #222: Lost at Sea? Yet You Haven't Left Port!
This is a common scenario for novice cruisers. Until you're familiar with the layout of your ship, take your ship layout plan/card with you. Also make a mental note of visual clues that'll help you find your cabin easier, such as a particular painting, decoration, stairwell or elevator.

Tip #223: Check Out the Library.
One of the first locations we like to check out on embarkation is

the library. This is where you might find a great read for your travels. Often, you'll also find board games that you can play should you be in the mood.

Tip #224: *Free Bottle of Wine? I'm In!*
Depending on the cruise line, you may be able to take advantage of certain incentives being offered on your first day of cruising. A typical scenario is that of being offered an incentive to dine in the ship's up-scale restaurant the first night. We do this on every Carnival cruise, as it not only gives us a free bottle of wine to enjoy with the meal, but we also enjoy the incredible pampering when we do dine in the up-scale alternative.

Tip #225: *Don't Discount the Specialty Restaurant Dining.*
If you're a "foodie" like us, then you'll want to experience a memorable, blow your taste buds off, extravaganza while onboard. We always make at least one reservation in a specialty restaurant. For a nominal $15 - $40 fee per person, you can create a lasting memory you'll be talking about for years. We do.

Tip #226: *That's Muster Station, Not Mustard Station.*
Just be aware that all cruise lines will conduct a Muster station drill. In this post pandemic age, you'll probably be expected to watch a video, get a code and enter that code at your assigned muster station. So, don't get too comfortable kicking back or prancing around your cabin stark naked. Also, don't think you can skip this all-important safety drill. Knowing where to go in case of an emergency at sea could save your life and those in your party.

Tip #227: *Turn Me Over Honey. I'm Done.*
Feeling roasted and fried to a crisp like a piece of burnt toast? It can happen quickly. Be mindful of the effects of sun and wind on

your body, especially if you're a white boy from northern Canada. We've seen so many first-timers burnt to a crisp after their first day out on the deck. While it's tempting to lather up and spend your day soaking up the sun, take breaks often to cool off. Makes a whole lot of sense, right?

15

WHAT TO DO ONBOARD

From gaining insights into the best features aboard ship to saving money on your wine purchases, these cruise hacks will help you make the most of your time onboard. You'll be able to control what type of day you desire, from relaxing on deck to prancing around like a little Jack Russell dog.

Tip #228: Insights Galore.
Talk to as many people as you can. People who love to cruise relish in the idea of sharing their tips and experiences. By listening to what tidbits of sage advice they're willing to share, you may be able to save yourself some time, money and/or frustration. This is especially so if you're wanting to make the most of your time in certain ports of call.

Tip #229: Meet and Greet Activities.
On the first or second night, most cruise lines usually organize a singles' meet and greet event at one of the bars or nightclubs. These venues can be a great start. Also, group activities like sports,

trivia quizzes and board games are great ways to get to meet and know people.

Tip #230: Get to Know Your Crew.

Connecting with members of the crew can make your onboard stay even that much more enjoyable. Your activity hosts or hostesses are all very approachable and extremely knowledgeable about the ship and how to make the most of your stay. Taking the time to chat with the crew can give you insights into which activities not to miss and what amenities the crew members value the most while onboard.

Tip #231: Don't Miss Out the Next Day!

Cruise lines offer a myriad of activities to do onboard that appeal to a wide range of audiences. Every evening a daily program will be left in your room for the next day's activities. Before you turn in for the night take a moment to highlight those activities that catch your attention the most. This'll make better use of your time while onboard, rather than leaving your schedule up to chance.

Tip #232: Early or Late Seating?

Consider booking an early seating so you can take in the early evening show. This becomes more of a factor when traveling with youngsters or the grandparents. Also, arrive early in the theatre so that you can find seating up front where the action is most prevalent. To pass the time while waiting, we like to take a board game or our Kindle readers.

Tip #233: I Can't Handle Them at Supper Anymore!

For the most part, your fellow cruisers tend to be pleasant and friendly people. Talking to total strangers can be a pleasurable and informative experience. However, sometimes you'll find table mates who don't fit your expectations. This has happened to us.

Should you happen to be at a table with people you don't like, then ask the Maître D' to change you to a different table. Doing so sooner, rather than later, increases the likelihood of your request being granted.

Tip #234: Isn't All the Food All-Inclusive?
Not quite. Your cruise ticket covers those meals offered in the main dining areas. However, all cruise ships have specialty restaurants that require you to pay a modest fee. They provide exceptional value should you like to tantalize your taste buds. Some of the specialty restaurants can be very popular, so try to book your seating in advance. Otherwise, you may be disappointed when you've set your heart on a particular dining experience and find out they're booked solid. We often pre-book any reservations online prior to our cruise departure.

Tip #235: How to Avoid the Food Rush.
Consider having your main meals before or after the normal peak meal hours. You'll find that the queues are much shorter. Not only that, when it's not super busy you get to pick the tables with the best views. We usually grab breakfast early so that we can take in the morning sunrise. We also try to snack throughout the day to avoid some of the lineups around lunchtime.

Tip #236: Scooby Snacks Anyone?
If you're wanting a late-night snack or something to nibble on while in port, grab a few items from the buffet and pack them into disposable plastic food containers or zip-lock bags. Then, should you get the munchies later in the evening, you won't have to leave your cabin to find something to eat.

Tip #237: The Room Service Alternative.
Most cruise ships offer a limited room service menu that is

complementary. You'll find the food selections somewhat average. Room service can be a good alternative for families with small children, instead of dealing with the challenge of getting them fed at a buffet or in a dining room when they're uncooperative. It's also expected that you'll tip the person who delivers your room service. A couple of bucks should do it.

Tip #238: Purchase Soft Drink, Specialty Coffee, Beer and Wine Packages Early.

These packages are typically available for purchase on the first couple of days of cruising. Buying a drink package in bulk can save you a lot of money, that's if you like to indulge. We like to book our packages online prior to sailing, so that we can spend more time enjoying the onboard amenities rather than having to make arrangements for the various packages on Day One.

Tip #239: Tip Your Servers Early. It's Well Worth It.

Take care of those who serve your food and drinks by tipping them early on your cruise. Doing so ensures that they'll go out of their way to please you and provide continued good service. A few dollars, goes a long way. They do notice and do care. You should tip for the future service you "want" to receive, as opposed to the service you "have" received. Does that make sense?

Tip #240: Get into the Thick and Thin of the Action.

There is an abundance of stage shows on every cruise. Many of the performers encourage audience participation. Arrive early and grab a seat up front near the stage steps. This not only increases your chances of getting picked, but you'll also enjoy the performance more by being right where the action is unfolding.

Tip #241: Be Adventurous! Try Something New.

You're on a cruise vacation. Now, it's time to have fun and relax.

Consider trying some different experiences, new cuisine and new entertainment. You never know what might tickle your fancy until you try, right? Keep in mind that doing nothing on a cruise is hard. You never know when you're finished.

Tip #242: All Hands on Deck! It's Movie Time.
Many cruise lines offer movies either on deck or in smaller show theatres. To make the most of your evening set up early with a blanket or warm apparel in case a cool wind picks up in the evening. You may even want to grab a small travel pillow for maximum comfort.

Tip #243: Want to Get Pampered at a Bargain?
Some of the best times to book a spa package are when the ship is in port. Most cruise guests will head out for the day to explore the local area. You can pick up some great bargains by booking early. Don't dilly-dally if you're considering booking some pampering, as spots fill up quickly.

Tip #244: Waiting to Grab a Shower?
Consider heading down to the fitness/ spa area and grabbing a shower there. With several individuals sharing the same cabin, coordinating bathroom access can be a challenge. The fitness facilities have more space to move around in and you'll be surprised at how many people don't take advantage of this hack. Wouldn't this be so much easier?

Tip #245: Enter Contests and Draws.
We've been lucky on recent cruises in having been selected for various spa services at a huge discount. Something to consider, right? Also, many of the games, such as trivial pursuit or golf putting that are organized by the ship, offer a trophy prize if you

can win it. Yes, you could be the proud owner of a plastic ship on a stick by being a winner.

Tip #246: Is This My Best Side?

Every cruise ship has a team of professional photographers taking photos throughout the day and evening. The photos will appear on photo walls for you to check out and possibly purchase. Be forewarned that the photos are quite tempting to buy, but are expensive. On your last night of your trip check back with the photo shop to see if they're having any last-minute special offers. You may be able to negotiate a better deal.

Tip #247: Shipboard Deals to Be Had?

Generally speaking you'll find shipboard prices on most items high. You can often get a better deal in your home city or by shopping online. However, you may wish to check out the daily specials onboard your cruise ship. These tend to be very popular, not unlike a Black Friday sale. As well, most ship-branded souvenir items do not come on sale, with the exception of some items like clothing or bags.

Tip #248: Oh My God! I Never Knew We Drank So Much.

Watch your expenditures on board. Avoid the sticker shock of receiving a bill at the end of your cruise that ends up costing you more than the cruise itself. With your sail card, there's no need to carry cash. You can easily forget how much money you're actually spending on booze or other items. Your best bet is to keep receipts of all of your purchases so that you can keep better track of your indulgences & expenditures. You can also keep tabs on your purchases online through the cruise ship's app.

Tip #249: Are You a Buff Bob?

Want to get a great workout in? Sign up for a spin bike or fitness class. Most cruise itineraries will have at least one day at sea where you won't be visiting a particular port of call. On these days, we enjoy popping into the fitness facility to get in some sort of a workout. It breaks up our day with some physical activity. Hitting Mach 2 on the water slide can only go so far in terms of burning off calories. And using the excuse that you get enough exercise by pushing your luck may not be the best strategy to adopt on a cruise that provides six square meals a day. Right?

Tip #250: Hot Tubs Are Not Hot.
Heads up on this one. Be forewarned that hot tubs located on deck are usually kept at body temperature so that patrons don't overindulge especially when alcohol is being served in the immediate area. If you're looking for a hotter soak, try the spa or fitness area. As well, most of the pools on deck will be saltwater filled meaning that they'll probably be at the temperature of the ocean, which is typically around 82 degrees in the Caribbean.

Tip #251: Are You a Wine Connoisseur?
Then, invest in the whole damn bottle. Buying individual drinks on cruise ships adds up quickly. If you love to drink wine, buy a bottle. What you don't consume at dinner can be corked and put aside for you for the next meal. As mentioned, consider investing in a beverage package which can be purchased online or on your first day of cruising. This'll save you a pretty penny down the road.

Tip #252: Can't Get Corked at This Price.
Avoid any corking fees should you decide to take your own bottle of wine to dinner by taking just a glass of wine from your cabin. We've often brought a couple of special bottles of wine along with us on a cruise. When the supper hour approaches, we'll pour a glass of wine to sip on while we're getting ready. Then, as we leave

for dinner we'll top up our glasses and head to the dining area. No need to pay for corkage fees.

Tip #253: Free Bubbly Anyone?

Sign up and show up for the art auction onboard and you may be treated to a glass or two of champagne. Who cares if you're not going to buy anything. You'll get to see the art, hear any discussions about the artist and/or pieces and have fun sipping on some bubbly. Not a bad way to spend a portion of your day, wouldn't you agree?

Tip #254: Buyer Beware. The Tax Man Cometh.

Shopping can be a lot of fun. However, the cruise lines make a significant portion of their profits from your onboard purchases and those you make in recommended shops. Avoid purchasing big ticket items. They're almost always less expensive back home by doing a little Internet investigating. Keep in mind that you'll need to pay U.S. Customs duties on expensive items you purchase above your personal exemption, which is around $800 in total goods.

16

MAKING THE MOST AT PORTS OF CALL

The world is your oyster. If you're adventurous, then exploring ports of call will be your cup of tea. The following cruise hacks walk you through what to expect when in port and give you some options to consider for making the most of your day.

Tip #254: The World Is Yours to Explore.
Go beyond the usual tourist traps by getting "outside" of the main cruise terminal area. Prior to your cruise vacation, Google each destination for interesting venues to explore while in port. Whether on your own or with a local guide, you'll find that by getting into the community you'll have a better appreciation of the culture and attractions.

Tip #255: Be Street Smart.
Cruise destinations are generally safe and friendly places. Robbery hold ups are uncommon. Lesser crimes such as pickpockets and bag snatchers do occur from time to time. Try not to be too flashy with your cash and valuables. Leave jewelry and expensive watches in your cabin.

When at the beach, make sure your belongings are tended to while you're in the water. I always carry a waterproof, plastic storage cylinder containing our cash around my neck when we do go for a dip. Something to consider getting, right?

Tip #256: A Little Local Language Goes a Long Way.
Use this tip for any foreign vacation. Learning a handful of common language phrases can help break down any communication barriers. It never ceases to amaze me when something as simple as a greeting or thank you can bring such a positive reaction. And don't forget to smile.

Tip #257: Get into the Tendering Draw Early.
If you would like to maximize your time on shore, pay attention to the ticketing start time for signing up for tenders. Tenders are the small boats used to shuttle cruise guests to shore. Grab your tickets as early as possible since queue numbers are allocated to guests on a first-come, first-served basis. Also, have your entire party go to collect ticket numbers, since all of your party members will need to be present in order to receive a queue number. Should you be on a cruise-sponsored excursion, you'll be given a specific tender time. Try to arrive early with your party in the staging area assigned for tendering.

Tip #258: Handling Foreign Currency.
The U.S. greenback is accepted as currency in most ports of call, along with the local currency. You'll often get a better deal on purchases if you're dealing in the local currency though. We like to take a number of small U.S. bills with us for inexpensive items and tips. If you do exchange some foreign currency, try to use up all the local coins if you can. When you try to exchange any leftover foreign currency after returning home, you'll find that most banks will not exchange those coins or small bills.

Tip #259: Anticipate Changes to the Weather.

Weather can be unpredictable. This is why we always pack rain gear that also serves as a windbreaker should an afternoon storm present itself in port. We'll also bring along another top either short-sleeved or long-sleeved depending on whether the day is getting cooler or warmer when out and about. Having some additional layers with us maximizes our time in port while staying comfortable. You don't want to be miserable, do you?

Tip #260: Taking a Taxi in Your Port of Call?

Always agree on a price "before" you get into the taxi or van. Get a verbal confirmation as to the total cost of the trip. It's important for your driver to agree to a total amount, including any tolls or charges you may not be aware of. It's quite possible you'll get overcharged for the ride if you're not clear upfront.

Tip #261: Renting a Scooter. Be Forewarned.

Bombing around ports of call and the countryside in a scooter can be fun. They're easy to rent. The downside is that they're also very easy to crash and cause a major injury. Be very careful should you consider this option. The danger is not in you driving the scooter, but rather other drivers hitting you. That would put a serious damper on your cruise, wouldn't it?

Tip #262: A Case for Cruise Organized Shore Excursions.

For convenience, security and peace of mind, this is a good option if this is your first cruise or if you have young children. Booking a cruise organized tour avoids any hassles and uncertainty. You'll be guided every step of the way. This is also a good option if the port is on a remote island where it's easy to get lost and public transport is non-existent.

Tip #263: DIY Organized Shore Excursions Might Be Better.
If your ship is docked at a major urban center, then the do-it-yourself option could be the way to go. You'll have more tour operators to choose from. And alternative transport is readily available in case the tour bus breaks down. Prior to your vacation, do your own extensive online research to identify those tour operators offering the best quality and value. Websites like **ShoreFox.com** should help narrow down your search.

Tip #264: Shopping at "Official" Stores in Port.
As you can imagine, shopping in a foreign country can be fun. A word of caution, though. Avoid making impulse purchases of expensive items, since you probably aren't getting as great a deal as you think. Be aware that shopping in Cruise Line Approved Stores is strongly promoted and recommended by the cruise line because they get paid to send you to those stores.

Tip #265: Attend Shopping Seminars Offered by the Cruise Ship.
You may not be interested in learning about all of the deals being promoted by the cruise ship at recommended shops. However, these informative sessions can give you a better feel as to how the port of call is laid out, what other attractions to visit and what to expect in port.

Tip #266: Duty Free Alcohol.
Should you purchase duty free alcohol onboard or in port, don't expect to be able to drink it while on your cruise. All alcohol purchases, both tax-free and regularly priced items are stored for safekeeping until disembarkation. This prevents you from drinking it onboard. Just know that the cruise lines prefer that you buy alcohol from their bars. Makes sense, right?

Tip #267: Cash is King.
Not every vendor or buying situation accepts credit cards or
traveller's checks. Save hassle time or embarrassment by bringing
some cash for tips, photos, souvenirs and even for lockers on
certain excursions. A handful of small bills should keep you
afloat.As previously mentioned, keep your cash close to your
person using an under-garment pouch, waterproof storage
cylinder or backpack worn on your back.

Tip #268: Pack a Scooby Snack and Water.
If you're heading out to explore a port of call for the day, take some
pastry and hard-boiled eggs with you. This'll help keep your
energy level up. You'll want to avoid taking any fruit as it may be
confiscated. As an alternative, you may prefer having a couple of
energy bars with you. To save money, bring a few bars along on
your trip from home.

Tip #269: Where am I going to put all this stuff?
We recommend taking a collapsible, lightweight backpack with a
capacity of around 30 Liters. Being able to drape your "day" bag
over your shoulders frees up your hands. Should you be going on
any adventurous excursions or if you end up walking any distance,
you'll appreciate having a backpack to carry your personal effects
more efficiently. And, what should you put in your backpack? We
almost always have the following with us:

1. A hydration system or 1 Liter plastic water bottle filled
   with ice water.
2. Sun screen.
3. Mosquito repellent (travel size bottle or wipes).
4. Sanitary hand wipes or small bottle of hand sanitizer.
5. Whistle.
6. Plastic bags for any wet gear.

7. Umbrella for the sun/ rain.
8. Reading material (Kindle reader or pocket book).
9. Snacks (usually from the cruise ship).
10. Personal identification, cash, credit card.
11. Digital camera/ iPad/ mobile phone.
12. Extra top for either cooler or warmer conditions as the day unfolds.

Then, depending on the activity we're doing in port we'll add in other items like beach towels and swimwear.

Tip #270: Keep Track of Your Time on Shore.
You're 100% responsible for getting back to the cruise ship before it sails when you explore ports of call on your own. If you're having a great time in a local bar or restaurant, don't lose track of time. Easy to do when you're having fun. Consider setting an alarm on your phone that warns you it's time to head back to the port. And make sure that you're following "ship time" as opposed to just the local time. Some cruise itineraries that cross time zones, don't adjust clocks to reflect the local time, but rather keep the clocks set to ship time.

17

STAYING CONNECTED

Trying to stay connected back home can be challenging when sailing in international waters. The following cruise hacks will help you not only save money, but also eliminate some common frustrations when using various devices.

Tip #271: Maybe It's Time to Unplug?
Communication with home is available, but it can be very expensive. Expect phone calls from your own cell phone to cost you $5 to $8 per minute. Internet and Data services on your phone will cost you about $15 per megabyte which is about $30 to $45 to upload one picture. And text messages are generally around 25 to 50 cents each. If you plan on using the Internet while cruising, be prepared to pay hefty prices for onboard Internet and roaming fees on your cellular device. Hence, the argument for taking a break from your devices.

Tip #272: Before Heading Out the Door on Your Cruise.
Your first order of business should be to set up an automatic reply for your email so that people know you're on vacation and you'll

get back to them later. Next, make sure to have your voice mail set up on your phone and that your inbox is empty, so that any recorded messages can be listened to later. Also consider downloading any digital entertainment to your personal devices so that you can use it offline.

Tip #273: What to Expect Using Your Computer or Tablet?
Many cruise lines have packages as low as $5 per day to access all the basic social media sites from your own devices. With some cruise lines, streaming video or music, like YouTube or Netflix will be frustrating. Both these services take up a lot of bandwidth, taking so long to load anything that it won't be worthwhile.

Video chat applications like Skype and FaceTime take up even more Internet data. Many cruise ships offering Internet services have a system that detects these applications and keeps them from working. Those that do support such applications will charge heavily for it, up to a dollar per minute of video chatting.

Tip #274: The Onboard Computers Are an Option.
Most cruise ships have computers located in internet or "cyber" cafes. You can pay for a certain amount of time to log onto one of the ship's computers, usually around a buck a minute. These cafes are a convenient way to access social media sites, check on email and do some light web surfing without having to bring your own device. Just ensure that you write down or memorize your usernames and passwords, as these computers won't automatically pre-fill this information like your computers at home might.

Tip #275: Best Times to Access the Internet?
Use any onboard services late at night or early in the morning, when fewer passengers will be using it. Speeds will usually be faster during these times as well.

Tip #276: Place Your Devices on Airplane Mode.
Cell phone companies charge expensive roaming fees when you travel outside of your coverage. Roaming charges for using cellular data on your mobile network are usually higher that the Internet packages offered by the cruise lines. To avoid these fees, turn off data roaming on your cell phone. Place your devices on airplane mode, but keep the Wi-Fi option on so that you can connect to wireless internet options when available.

Tip #277: Setting up International Roaming.
Should you like to determine how much your cell phone provider could be charging you for international phone calls, dial 611 on your phone. Most cell phone providers can be reached at this number. Just ensure you do so before you head out to sea. As well, you could ask them to turn on "international roaming". This reduces the cost per minute from about $5 to $1.50. Something to consider, right?

Tip #278: "Copy, Paste, Send", to Save Money.
Should you need to stay in touch back home with friends or family via email try to spend as little time as possible online. Do so by writing your messages using a word processor. Then, copy and paste them into your email platform to quickly send them off. The same strategy applies to responding to emails. Copy and paste your incoming messages, then read your messages once offline. Your goal? Minimize your time spent connecting to the Internet.

Tip #279: Use Kindle "Whispernet" to Send Free Emails.
If you have a Kindle device that can use Whispernet, you may be able to send and receive emails through your web browser that is included with your Kindle. You can access a standard email account through services like Google Gmail or Yahoo. When it works, it's free. More often than not, it'll be slow.

Tip #280: Free Wi-Fi in Ports?
Ask members of your crew where the best places to go for free Internet are at each port, as they use these services themselves to stay in touch with family and friends as they travel. Tourist welcome booths, which are usually one of the first buildings you'll pass as you disembark, will also point you in the right direction as to where the best places for Wi-Fi are.

Wi-Fi hotspots, Internet cafes, coffee shops and restaurants offering Internet services can be found all over ports of call. We wary of places that advertise that they have the best Internet connection for the best price. These may be tourist traps. You could end up paying extreme rates, or have to buy their products or services to access the Internet.

Tip #281: Using VOIP (Voice over Internet Protocol).
Connecting your phone to the ship's Wi-Fi and using VOIP, such as Skype, Vonage or Google Voice, will probably cost you about the same as dialing direct, which should be about $1 per minute. rather than paying over $5 per minute. It's best to choose to connect with VOIP through your computer using the Internet (rather than cell service), which gives you more flexibility. And, be forewarned VOIP service may be blocked on certain cruise lines.

Tip #282: Need to Work? Think of a Tablet.
Consider taking a tablet with a keyboard attachment. Not only will you save space, but it'll be a lot easier traveling with your mobile office when at the airport, in ports of call, lounging on the deck, etc. Since I'm often working while vacationing, this option allows me greater flexibility than a laptop, which can be cumbersome at times when traveling.

Tip #283: Hidden Outlets?
If your stateroom has limited electrical outlets, take a look at your TV. Many TV sets have a USB port, which you can use as an extra outlet to charge your electronic devices. We often have two cell phones, two iPads, and two Kindle readers on the go when we vacation. So, this is often a good option for us, even when we're in a hotel room.

Tip #284: Use the Shipboard App.
Most cruise lines have their own app that's connected to the ship's Wi-Fi. The app generally allows you to check onboard account balances, browse the day's activity schedule, check out dining room menus, and even make reservations. Download the app for free to your cellphone or tablet. If you don't already own walkie-talkies, this is a more affordable option for the infrequent cruiser. For a modest fee of around $8 - $10, you can communicate with fellow passengers through your cellphone.

Tip #285: Book Your Onboard Wi-Fi Package Online and Save.
In most cases buying Wi-Fi before you embark on your cruise can save you money. Granted, not every cruise line offers discounts. However, an online booking could save you 10-15% for those that do advertise or promote this type of incentive.

18

YOUR LAST DAY

What should you expect on your last day of cruising? There'll be a lot on your plate on your last day at sea. Making the most of your day while attending to debarkation matters is the focus of the following cruise hacks.

Tip #286: Charge Your Mobile Devices Beforehand.
After so many days at sea, your mobile phone battery will probably be flat or near-flat if you haven't been using it. So, give it and any other mobile devices a full charge the night before so that they'll be ready for use when you leave the ship.

Tip #287: Look for Bargains.
Save some of your onboard shopping until the last day of your cruise. Cruise lines often put more items on sale at this point in time. You may be able to pick up that souvenir plastic ship on a stick at a bargain. Now, we're talking!

Tip #288: Make Someone's Day.
And, we're not talking about Arnold Schwarzenegger's famous

line. It's a nice touch at the end of your cruise to leave staff members who you've connected with a little thank you card. A simple, inexpensive card that expresses your appreciation goes a long way in making a real difference in the lives of those who have made you vacation a memorable one.

Tip #289: Tipping Those Who Have Made Your Stay Enjoyable.
If you haven't been given (or taken) the option to have tips automatically charged to your account, now is the time to do so. Plan on giving your cabin steward and main waiter around $3.50 per day per person ($25 per week) and your assistant waiter around $2.00 per day per person ($15 per week). Expect to pay around $10 per day per person ($75 per week) at a minimum. They've worked long hard hours to make your vacation a pleasurable one. It's time to reward those efforts.

Tip #290: Leave Positive Reviews in Your Survey.
Complaining about a particular crew member (unless they had a significant negative impact on your vacation) or even leaving an average rating, could result in them losing their livelihood down the road. On the flip side, if someone has done an outstanding job, take a moment to mention their name in your survey. It'll go a long way to making them feel special.

Tip #291: Scrutinize Your Final Statement as Soon as Possible.
If you haven't been verifying your onboard purchases on a daily basis, ensure that you check your final statement early rather than later. Should you have questions or spot a problem, you could end up standing in a long line waiting your turn to resolve an issue. Also, once you have your final statement, ensure that you keep a copy for your records should a dispute arise down the road involving your credit card company.

Tip #292: Be Like Sherlock Holmes When You Pack.

This is an obvious hack. Make sure to double check your drawers, closet shelves, the safe and under your bed when packing to leave. It's easy to miss small, valuable items that may go unnoticed until it's too late. We left a pair of expensive gold earrings on a shelf on one of our cruises. It was a stressful process reconnecting with the earrings. Not something you want to experience, wouldn't you agree?

Tip #293: Pack Leisurely Throughout the Day.

Avoid the mad rush in the evening trying to pack everything at the last minute. Your goal should be to maximize your time enjoying the last night's festivities and activities. If you're stuck in your room having to pack your bags at the last minute you defeat this purpose and could miss out on some memorable experiences. Wouldn't that be a bummer?

Tip #294: Using the Luggage Carry Service?

A day or so before disembarkation, you'll be given a form to fill out specifying whether or not you would like your luggage carried off the ship for you to the customs area. Should you opt to use the luggage carry service, your bags must be collected the night before disembarkation.

You'll have the convenience of not having to drag your bags off the ship. The downside is that you don't have access to all of your luggage the night before. This is why we often prefer the self-carry option. And is yet another reason why we strive to pack light.

Tip #295: Plan on Being Out of Your Cabin by 8:30 a.m.

The morning of your departure will be an early one, especially if you've had a habit of sleeping in during your stay. Expect to have everything out of your cabin by 8:30 at the latest, so that the crew can turn the ship around for the next cruise guests. This means ensuring that you grab a bite to eat as early as possible.

Tip #296: Hurry Up and Wait!

You could end up spending a considerable amount of time waiting to be called to leave the ship. To help pass the time and make the most of the morning before departure, we read or play one of our board games while waiting to be kicked off the ship. It beats twiddling your thumbs and staring at the ceiling, wouldn't you agree? Unless that's something that turns your crank.

19

HANDLING PROBLEMS & CONCERNS

Finally, in this chapter, we'll address some common issues that may be of concern particularly when you're on a cruise. The remaining cruise hacks should provide you with a sense of relief in knowing how to best cope with certain problems that could arise.

Tip #297: How to Avoid Minor illness.
Keep your immune system healthy and strong prior to and during your trip. This means pacing yourself, getting plenty of rest and staying hydrated. When you exhaust yourself all the time and don't drink enough water (sorry, beer doesn't quite cut it), your immune system slows down leaving you more vulnerable to illness. You'll also want to avoid food that is lukewarm, especially if it's supposed to be especially hot or cold. And, try to drink bottled water while you explore the ports.

Tip #298: Preventing COVID-19, Norovirus and Zika.
Practice good hygiene everywhere you go. Wash your hands frequently and use the hand sanitizers that the ship provides to

avoid picking up anything off of railings, doors, chairs and tabletops. COVID has drastically changed how the cruise lines feed and entertain their patrons. Constant sanitizing greatly decreases your chances of catching any contagious virus. Also, when you head into ports of call, plan on taking a few personal hygiene items with you, such as a small bottle of hand sanitizer, protective masks, toilet paper, small hand towel or some wet naps.

Tip #299: Motion Sickness Remedies.
Prevention is your first line of defence. Avoid spending long periods of time inside, below deck and away from any windows. You're not a mushroom, right? Get into the habit of getting fresh air regularly and looking out over the horizon to fend off any dizziness. Given the choice, use acupressure wrist bands rather than drugs that could make you drowsy when dealing with any motion sickness. You could also sit in the hot tub or pool until the queasiness disappears. Some cruisers like to eat a few dry biscuits as a quick relief. Or, they'll nibble on snacks containing ginger to help fight the nausea. If you are particularly prone to motion sickness, ensure that you drink plenty of water, and stay mid-ship if possible, where it rocks less than the front or back. Keep in mind that what may work for one person, might not do a thing for another. This is why having a number of seasickness remedies on hand stacks the odds in your favor to find a solution.

Tip #300: Noise Solutions.
A constant barrage of loud, high energy music can get annoying after a while. You may be able to get a reprieve if you head to a more serene location like the ship's library or one of the quieter adult-only areas. Should noise be an issue for us, we prefer using a set of ear plugs and/or noise-cancelling headphones to dampen the sound. Also, when we do book a balcony cabin, we have the

option of sitting outside in a quieter environment should we desire some peace and quiet.

Tip #301: Dealing with Crime and Theft.

Cruise ships are equipped with their own security personnel and video camera networks that focus on the public areas. Serious crime is not common on cruise ships, but do take some precautions and protect yourself. Avoid walking alone late at night. As they say, there's safety in numbers. Minor crime, like pickpocketing, in port cities is more common, which is why you should keep your jewelry back in your cabin and have any valuable items like cash, credit cards and ID attached to your body. This could be in a backpack strapped to your back or a travel wallet that you wear under your clothing.

Tip #302: Handling Aggressive Vendors.

Salesmen and vendors in certain ports of call can be very persistent and bothersome, especially in some ports. It can be aggravating to say the least. One word of advice: Don't sweat petty things ... or pet sweaty things. In Mexico, aggressive vendors aren't usually a big problem, but in Jamaica it's rampant. You'll find that you can avoid these individuals more easily when booked on cruise sponsored tours and shore excursions. Should you be confronted, firmly and politely tell them no, you're not interested in anything they're offering. Keep the conversation short and to the point. If possible, avoid eye contact when approached.

Tip #303: Credit Card Issues.

Credit card problems can occur at the worst possible times. More often than not, the credit card company may freeze your account if they suspect any illegal transactions. This is why being proactive and notifying your credit card provider of your travel plans helps. Not only are they aware of any unusual or foreign transactions, they also know in advance that you're traveling thus making it easier to support your case should you run into problems. Consider taking at least two credit cards that have sufficient limits to cover your necessary expenses. This'll provide you with a backup if one doesn't work. When you do get back home, pay attention to the details on your credit card statement and contact your provider immediately should you see any major discrepancies.

Tip #304: Create Lasting Memories.
As a final parting tip, this is one that resonates with us the most. Whenever we vacation, we make every effort to capture those special moments that are memorable. Whether we take photos or video of our exploits and adventures on our own, or purchase photos that resonate with us the most, we make a point of having something back home that'll trigger those special memories. Some of our best cruises have been the ones that we were able to relive in the comfort of our home. Strive to do the same.

AFTERWORD

When you embark on a cruise for the very first time, you're taking your first steps toward a wonderful new experience. Even though you may be on board a ship, your journey is filled with endless possibilities. Cruise ships are in the business of making sure that you're entertained, relaxed, and well taken care of. No longer do you need to worry about long drives each day of your vacation, booking hotel rooms every night, or organizing your meals throughout the day. You'll be able to see the world while in the comfort of your cabin.

The cruise hacks that I have shared with you, should help you kick back, relax and unwind. You'll be able to treat yourself to the spa, beauty salon and fine dining should you choose. You get to control what type of day you'll have, from being active exploring all that cruising activities and excursions have to offer to just experiencing the joy of watching the ocean sail by.

I hope that you've been able to pick up at least one cruise tip that'll help you create those lasting memories. Have fun planning your next cruise vacation. And don't worry if Plan A fails, there are 25 more letters in the alphabet.

Review Request:

Before you go, I'd like to thank you for investing in my guide. I know that you could have picked from dozens of books offering cruise tips, but you took a chance with my guide. So, a big thank you for selecting this book and reading all the way to the end.

If you enjoyed this book or if you found that you've gained greater insights into how you could conceivably make the most of your cruise, then I'd be very grateful if you'd post a positive review on Amazon.

Your support really does matter and it really does make a difference. The feedback and encouragement will help me continue to write the kind of books that help you get results. If you'd like to leave a review then all you need to do is go to the **Customer Review** section on the book's Amazon page. You'll then see a big button that says: "**Write a Customer Review**" - click that and you're good to go.

Thanks again for your support. Enjoy your next memorable cruise vacation.

Randall

$\sim$

MEET RANDALL

Randall is a fun-loving, espresso-drinking, outdoor enthusiast who has travelled extensively across North America, the Caribbean and Europe.

His love of teaching has taken him into the corporate world, universities and public-school systems across Canada. He holds Bachelor degrees in both Education and Physical Education. Randall was instrumental in changing how language programs were being delivered in the business world in Quebec where he had a language and communication company geared towards creating tailor-made courses.

Since retiring from the teaching profession, Randall has been developing multi-media online programs for the financial and health care arenas. He loves seeing others develop healthy lifestyle habits that have a huge impact on the quality of their lives. This fuels his personal passion for sharing his interests in fitness and using more natural approaches to managing one's health challenges.

When Randall is not having fun learning about his passions for travel, the wine industry and the health sector, he can be found hiking, mountain biking, kayaking and cross-country skiing in the Pacific Northwest with his wife Cindy. When they're taking some down time, you'll see them enjoying the outdoors by being physically active in the company of Mother Nature, whether it be exploring extensive underground cave systems in Cancun, horseback riding in the ocean in Jamaica, or scuba diving off the coast of the Grand Caymans.

They've also been known to sip on the occasional glass of Barolo wine with good friends while preparing some of their favorite Italian dishes. Above all - they enjoy living life to the fullest and creating lasting memories. They hope that this guide will empower you to do the same.

DISCLAIMER

This book was produced with the goal of providing information that is as accurate and reliable as possible. Regardless, purchasing this book can be seen as consent to the fact that both the publisher and the author of this book are in no way experts on the topics discussed within and that any recommendations or suggestions that are made herein are for entertainment purposes only. Professionals should be consulted as needed prior to undertaking any of the action endorsed herein.

This declaration is deemed fair and valid by both the American Bar Association and the Committee of Publishers Association and is legally binding throughout the United States.

Furthermore, the transmission, duplication or reproduction of any of the following work including specific information will be considered an illegal act irrespective of if it is done electronically or in print. This extends to creating a secondary or tertiary copy of the work or a recorded copy and is only allowed with express written consent from the Publisher. All additional rights reserved.

Disclaimer

The information presented is broadly considered to be a truthful and accurate account of facts and as such any inattention, use or misuse of the information in question by the reader will render any resulting actions solely under their purview. There are no scenarios in which the publisher or the original author of this work can be in any fashion deemed liable for any hardship or damages that may befall them after undertaking information described herein.

Additionally, the information in this book is intended only for informational purposes and should thus be thought of as universal. As befitting its nature, it is presented without assurance regarding its prolonged validity or interim quality. Trademarks that are mentioned are done without written consent and can in no way be considered an endorsement from the trademark holder.

Made in the USA
Las Vegas, NV
28 July 2021